Active Learning:

A Practical Guide for College Faculty

Introduction by Maryellen Weimer, PhD

MAGNA

Madison, Wisconsin

Magna Publications
2718 Dryden Drive
Madison, WI 53704
Magnapubs.com

Some articles in this book have been previously published in *The Teaching Professor* newsletter, *Online Classroom* newsletter, *Faculty Focus*, or have been adapted from Magna Online Seminars or 20-Minute Mentor presentations.

ISBN: 978-0-912150-61-1

Contents

Introduction

Maryellen Weimer, PhD

Active learning is now a mainstay of teaching in higher education and for a convincing set of reasons. Learning by doing trumps learning by listening. There's just too much evidence to conclude otherwise. Yes, there's still a place for lecture; some content is better explained than discovered. But active learning is about dealing directly with the content, connecting it to and with what is already known, and figuring out how it applies. Learning is an active process and teachers need to use approaches, activities, and assignments that get students involved and engaged with course content, with learning, and with each other.

And here's just the collection to help teachers do that. It starts where most teachers do with discussion and participation. These are the go-to active learning strategies and for good reasons. Talking about the content can accomplish a number of important outcomes. Saying out loud what you know and understand about something clarifies your thinking about it. It provides both the learner and the teacher feedback as to the levels of understanding. Talking about the content gives students a chance to practice learning the vocabulary of the discipline. It's motivating when they hear themselves sounding a bit like professionals. And student contributions in class, online or in discussions, develop important communication skills. The various articles in this section provide ideas and information as to how participation and discussion can be used to accomplish these goals.

One of the benefits of several decades' worth of interest in active learning is a plethora of activities and assignments that can be used to promote it. In the second section, this collection offers range of different examples that are widely applicable across disciplines and in different kinds of courses. Any active learning approach does need to be tailored to fit the particulars of the situation where it will be used. So, collections like this one should be viewed as an introduction to what's possible. They describe activities and assignments that can be changed slightly or significantly so that they work well given the content, the teacher's style, and the learning needs of students.

Group work has proven itself an effective way to get students dealing with the content and each other. Much research, across many disciplines, verifies that students can learn from and with each other in groups. However, those learning outcomes do not accrue automatically. Careful attention must be paid to how the groups are formed, how long they interact, group size, the kind of tasks that work in one class session as opposed to projects worked on throughout the course, group dynamics issues, and finally how the learning is assessed when it occurs in collective contexts. All these issues and more are addressed by material in the third section.

One distinct advantage of Magna Publications material resources: they contain succinct readable pieces. Most teachers don't have time to wade through lengthy, detailed journal articles. Teachers need to know the essential point and where they can learn more if the topic is of interest. Here's a collection with articles that can be read individually or collectively, in five minutes or in an afternoon.

Active learning isn't a new idea—John Dewey recommended it at the front end of the 20th century. What we have now at the beginning of the 21st century is a multitude of ideas and information on this important topic. This resource collection illustrates how much we have learned about making learning active.

Maryellen Weimer, PhD has edited The Teaching Professor *newsletter since 1987 and writes the Teaching Professor blog each week on* Faculty Focus. *She is a professor emerita of teaching and learning at Penn State Berks and won Penn State's Milton S. Eisenhower award for distinguished teaching in 2005.*

PART 1

•

Discussion and Participation

Three Tips for Navigating Contentious Classroom Discussions

Rob Dornsife, PhD

Reason to read: Disagreement, argument, and debate can play influential roles in learning, but only when the exchange moves forward productively. The author shares tips that will help to turn contentious moments into teaching moments.

Good teaching often relies on productive classroom discussion. However, many of us have experienced dynamics in which our discussions take a perilous turn and a palpable tension settles over the class. The precipitating comment may have offered a provocative perspective on an issue—maybe it rather aggressively challenged something someone said, or perhaps it smacked of racism, sexism, or some other discriminatory innuendo. Generally, students respond to comments they perceive as contentious with an awkward, uncomfortable silence. Nobody says anything; body language registers a collective recoil. What can or should teachers do when situations like this occur? Constructive disagreement, argument, and debate can play instrumental roles in learning, but not unless the exchange moves forward constructively. I'd like to offer three suggestions that can help teachers safely navigate through the potentially destructive terrains of contentious comments.

Remember that student investment is a crucial and desired resource. In my experience, contention in our classrooms usually results because the student cares. He or she has an investment in the idea or what's happened. Even contributions that are emotionally charged are offered because someone feels moved. We would first do well that caring engagement is a better and more readily engaged resource than complacency or indifference. So our first step toward navigating contention is to recognize that, more often than not, it results from a willingness to invest and engage. As such, it is a resource to be harnessed, not a tension to be feared.

Acknowledge the contention and define it as positively as possible. How we define such occurrences goes a long way toward determining how they are received. I often end an animated and perilous discussion by stating overtly how fortunate we are to have classmates this invested in what we are discussing and how this kind of caring is at the root of our shared inquiry. Crucial to this step is not ignoring or brushing aside contention, pretending that we all agree when we don't, or that our disagreements are small and inconsequential. Doing so risks heightening the negative dynamics. Taking a moment or two to say something like "the energy and investment demonstrated by your contributions is really what this class should be all about" redefines what may otherwise be seen as something to be avoided rather than anticipated as the class proceeds.

Use good spirit and humor to defuse contentious contributions. I have found that well-placed, supportive humor defuses most potentially negative energy. I recently had a young woman heatedly take issue with the comments a young man made in the class. What followed was one of those silent gasps literally felt around the room. My default reaction is respectful and honest humor. In this case, by combining suggestion two with this one, I said something like "Wow, Mary, you really care about this. We need to further unpack why and how this matters—and you are clearly up to that task. But in the meantime I would hate to lose to you in a poker game! Now let's explore what you've said and why it matters." I believe that humor often helps in these tense situations.

Though often overlooked, the beginning and the ending of class affords teachers some special opportunities. They are more casual times when we can frame what will happen or has happened in class. For example, if part of the class has taken one side and another part has taken the opposite position and gone after each other pretty aggressively, I have said as they leave class that I'll buy the coffee if they'd like to meet and talk through the issues more informally. Or, as the next class session begins, I may remark on how our previous discussion really made me think and that I found it stimulating and look forward to further engaged exchanges as the course proceeds.

These tips will not address the rare and extreme circumstances that require different interventions. However, in my experience, such responses enable us to constructively handle the majority of those contentious moments, transforming them into the healthy clash of different ideas and viewpoints we look forward to and depend on.

RECOMMENDED REFERENCE:

Monde, G. C. (2016). "Embracing tension in the classroom." *The Teaching Professor (30)*7.

Reprinted from *The Teaching Professor* newsletter, February 2016.

Does Participation Promote Engagement?

Maryellen Weimer, PhD

Reason to read: You may be surprised to hear what communication researchers have discovered about participation and engagement.

Most teachers would answer yes. It's one of the reasons they want students to participate. Whether they're paying attention because the teacher may call on them, or whether the questions and answers being exchanged have piqued their interest, participation keeps students engaged.

Communication education researchers Frymier and Houser point out those assumptions are prevalent not just among teachers, but within the literature as well. "A close reading of the literature on student participation reveals the assumption that students who orally participate in class are engaged in learning, and quiet students are less so" (p. 83). They report the results of two studies that challenge these widely held assumptions. The problem begins with how participation and engagement are used pretty much interchangeably. Frymier and Houser contend they are not equivalent constructs. "Participation is a component of engagement, while engagement is a multidimensional construct encompassing several student characteristics and behaviors" (p. 84). The research questions raised by the participation-engagement relationship are straightforward (p. 84): "Is oral participation really an indicator of engagement? Can quiet students be engaged?"

This survey research involved 674 students in the first study and 414 in the second. These students answered questions about the instructor and course they'd had immediately preceding the communication course during which the data were collected, which meant students were answering about a wide variety of instructors and across a range of disciplines. Both study designs are complex, involving measures of participation, communication apprehension, motivation to study, indicators of learning, engagement, and instructor nonverbal immediacy. All of these measures were empirically developed and had been used extensively in other research. In the second study, the participation measure was modified and a measure of classroom nonverbal attentiveness was developed. Data analysis methods are fully explained in the article.

As for findings, here's the most important one: "Study Two confirmed the first study; at best there is a slight relationship between oral participation and engagement…The correlations were small, leading us to conclude that oral participation is not a good indicator of engagement" (p. 99).

There were also some findings of interest related to grading participation, starting with the fact that in Study One, students reported it was graded in 57 percent of their courses and not graded in 43 percent of the courses. When it was graded, students reported that they participated more. And participation was associated with motivation to study and learning indicators. "Perhaps engaging in oral participation makes students feel like they are learning more; certainly students are told over and over that participation is the hallmark of a good student" (p. 92). However, the lack of connection between participation and engagement contains some indication that students are simply complying with teacher expectations. If the teacher expects them to speak, students "will find something to say during class" (p. 92). Moreover, participation was negatively correlated with communication apprehension, meaning anxious students reported participating less. "Oral participation is likely beneficial for students who have low CA (communication apprehension) and higher levels of willingness to communicate" (p. 100).

The second study revealed an alternative way of encouraging participation independent of grading it. Studied at length in the communication education field, teacher nonverbal immediacy has been consistently found to be positively associated with a number of different student outcomes. When teachers smile, establish eye contact with students, and move comfortably around the classroom space, the motivation for learning increases. In this case, "immediate teaching likely invites interaction and creates a more pleasant classroom climate than does tracking and grading participation" (p. 99). In these inviting classroom climates, students are more likely to communicate because they want to, rather than because they have to. In this research, instructor nonverbal immediacy was positively associated with student nonverbal attentiveness and oral participation.

Finally, this research documented that something other than participation was positively related to engagement: nonverbal attentiveness. As operationally defined by the measure developed for this research, nonverbal attentiveness included these items, among others: giving people complete attention when they are speaking, maintaining eye contact with people who are speaking in class, and responding nonverbally with head nods and facial expressions. "If instructors are trying to gauge the level of student engagement, the results of this study indicate they should rely more on students' nonverbal behaviors than their oral behaviors" (p. 99). There's another important implication here as well. Silent students are not always disengaged. Those who are listening may be learning even more than those who are speaking.

"The results of these studies challenge the long-held assumption that oral participation is unquestionably a good thing. It also suggests instructors need to rethink their grading of oral participation. If participation is the desired outcome, there may be other ways to encourage it" (p. 101).

RECOMMENDED REFERENCE:

Frymier, A. B., and Houser, M. L., (2016). The role of oral participation in student engagement. *Communication Education, 65* (1), 83–104.

Reprinted from *The Teaching Professor* newsletter, April 2016.

Reminders for Improving Classroom Discussion

Roben Torosyan, PhD

Use short, ungraded writing to deepen thinking (and to let people prepare before speaking up):

- Have students write for five minutes, then have them read their writing aloud, or list their main ideas on the board.
- For homework, have students write the questions they have about the reading. "What are you wondering about? What does this make you think of?"
- Use helpers to free yourself up to notice more discussion dynamics. Have a volunteer note questions on the board or flip chart (number them for reference).
- Ask questions vulnerably by wondering aloud, not knowing. Put on the board or in a PowerPoint document a question for which you don't have the answer.

Slow the flow, probe deeper:

- Use groups and assign each a different question, problem, or section of reading to report on.
- Probe for more meaning by extending wait time, repeating the question, and asking for more:
  "What did you say, Melanie? Hmm, interesting—why do you think that?"
  "Good. Can you say what your reasoning is?"
- Ask people to "say back" the opposing view to the other's satisfaction before they disagree.
- Transfer responsibility away from you to class:
  "Mmm—hmm. What is John getting at?"
  "If you can't hear someone, what can you do?"
  "Others, what does that mean to you?"
- FYI: Most teachers wait less than one second after asking a question. Increasing the wait to three to five seconds yields more and fuller responses, as well as more spontaneous speaking up, use of evidence, and student questions.

Balance students' voices:
- "Others we've heard from less?"
- "If it's already been said, how would you say it?"
- "Whose opinion on this topic would you like to hear?"
- Regularly remind students: "No question is stupid." (Say it so much that you as teacher sound stupid.)

Track themes to bring discussion back on track or reframe it:
- Nudge a group to move on: "Why don't we look at the fourth question you put on the board now?"
- Prompt for links: "Wait, what was the connection between this and Jack's question?"
- Use evidence to support or challenge ideas: "Do these lines answer Kanisha's question?"
- Offer your own dawning discoveries to encourage reframing: "Oh, I just realized! Maybe Hector is the real hero of the poem." "What if we solved the problem this way?"

Comment explicitly on group dynamics:
- "Please, folks, I can't hear her." "Let her finish." "One at a time."
- "How could we make this discussion better?"
- "What can we do to encourage those reluctant to contribute to share their thoughts?"
- At midterm, email individuals, "I'd really like to hear from you more in class. As your writing shows, others could gain from the greater diversity you'd bring. Participation counts too . . ."

Summarize what was learned (while valuing uncertainty, depending on the content):
- "Did you learn anything, or are you left thinking about anything?"
- "What struck you?" "What do you want to remember?"
- In general, use open questions ("what" and "why") over closed questions ("Is this clear?" or "Does that make sense?") to give practice at putting complex ideas into language.
- At end of class, give a "minute paper" or ask for the "muddiest point" and begin the next discussion by reviewing what students wrote about the previous one.

RECOMMENDED REFERENCES:

Brookfield, S. D., & Preskill, S. (1999). *Discussion as a Way of Teaching: Tools and Techniques for Democratic Classrooms*. San Francisco: Jossey-Bass.

Finkel, D. L. (2000). *Teaching with Your Mouth Shut*. Portsmouth, NH: Boynton/Cook.

Torosyan, R. From Controversy to Empathic Discourse. Resources posted at: www.faculty.fairfield.edu/rtorosyan.

Reprinted from *The Teaching Professor* newsletter, November 2006.

How Do I Include Introverts in Class Discussion?

Nicki Monahan, MEd

Reason to read: Every classroom likely includes introverted students. Here's how to identify them and respect their needs and preferences while still keeping them engaged.

Would you prefer to go to a party with 50 exciting, brand-new people that you've never met before, or would you prefer to have dinner with an old, dear friend? You've probably guessed already that extroverts would prefer the party and introverts would prefer dinner with a friend. But what does this have to do, in particular, with learning and students in our classroom discussions? Temperament influences our preferences for learning, and introverts have particular preferences about how they would choose to learn.

Not only is it a matter of preference, but it's also a matter of where introverts produce their best work and the conditions under which they are best suited for learning. Introverted students tend to be very comfortable with solitary learning. They're comfortable doing their learning through reading, research, writing, and sitting in a large lecture hall listening to someone.

Introverts are usually quite happy being alone, so the kinds of learning that lets them participate on their own are within their comfort zone. It's also typical of introverts to prefer to have some time to think before they speak. And in that thinking, they have an opportunity to sort out their thoughts, clarify their own thinking, and come to some creative kinds of thinking and some deep reflections.

Many introverts are comfortable using written formats to clarify their thinking. They like to write things down before they're asked to share them, and those writing opportunities allow them to think through the subject before speaking. Knowing these preferences and understanding the kinds of learning strategies that bring about the best results for introverts is important to us as faculty members.

To sum up introversion, it's really a matter of difference. A good analogy might be to think about the difference between left-handed people and right-handed people. One is not better than the other. One is not right, and the other is not wrong. They're simply differences, but they're differences that have implications. And as left-handed folks have had to try to learn how to live in a world that might be designed for right-handed people, so too do introverts in our classrooms sometimes struggle to feel like they should be more extroverted.

Technology options for introverts

The first option is online discussions. Introverts sometimes thrive in an online discussion forum situation because they have time. They have time to read other students' posts. They have time to think about what they might like to say in response. They may have time to do some reading and connect their reading to their online discussion post. And they certainly have time to write before posting.

An online discussion forum can be a good addition, one that's really within the comfort zone and the learning style of more introverted students. Many of today's faculty have started using Twitter, and many of our students are very comfortable with social media. Twitter is a quick way for students to respond in 140 characters to a point that could be made in class or to a discussion that's happening, and many introverted students are quite comfortable using Twitter as an informal way of contributing to a discussion. You could show the tweets up on your projection screen, or the exercise could be something that happens before, after, or between classes.

Nontech options for introverts

There are some nontech or no-tech options as well that really do give opportunities for students on the introverted end of the spectrum to participate without having to raise their hand and contribute in a large-class discussion.

Exit passes are a simple tool. This might be something that the faculty member designs and gives out to all students in class, something the students need to pass in before the end of the class as they leave the room or the lecture hall. On your exit pass, you might have formulated a question. You might ask students to respond to something that interested them in the day's discussion. Or you might ask them to apply something they've read to the conversation that just took place in class. It's an easy way to capture the ideas of students who may be engaged in class but who aren't raising their hands to participate.

Secondly, cue cards are a simple option to find out what's going on in the heads of those introverted students who aren't talking in your class-room. You can use a set of 3x5 cue cards, one for each class, and, again, there are some options. The faculty member may ask students to summarize in 3–5 sentences the key ideas from that day's class, or they could be asked to respond to reading or connect readings with the day's discussion, a very simple technique that enlarges the number of students participating in the discussion.

Finally, many faculty members use question boxes and, again, this tool is a great one for introverted students to share their questions that might come up during a class discussion but that they may be reluctant to raise their for hand and speak about. I like to use question boxes on a break in the middle of class. If we've had a conversation partway through class, as students are going to take their break, I ask them to put a question in their question box, and I take a few minutes to look at them on the break and respond.

All of these methods are great ways for students who are on the intro-verted end of the spectrum to contribute without having to raise their hands in a large class, something that might be well beyond their comfort zone. However, just as we want our students to build upon their strengths, we also want our students to develop new skills and to grow. I'd like to suggest some strategies that you can use to encourage verbal participation in class discussions from all students but especially introverts, who may be less com-fortable sharing in a large-group setting.

These are suggestions that might take students out of their comfort zone, encourage them to stretch, but we need to do that with some support. It's important to think about what happens on day one of any given class. If you don't establish norms, they get established for themselves. So it's important to think about who does the talking on the first day. If the fac-ulty member is the only one doing the talking, and you come back on the second week and are surprised that no one is contributing verbally to your discussions, it may be because unwittingly you set a norm on day one that faculty members do the talking and not students.

On the first day of class, it's important that you give students an opportunity to join the conversation. For introverted students, that might feel daunting, but if you use a developmental approach, it's something that they can certainly do with some support.

Partnered activities are a great place to begin, and even the most introverted students are likely to be comfortable if you simply ask them to turn to the person next to them, review the syllabus, come up with one idea that they share in common from the content that they're both interested in, and between the two members come up with a question about the syllabus—maybe about your participation policy.

Partnered activities are a great way to communicate, and in your class, everybody will contribute. Everybody has something to say, and everybody will do that right from the first day. It's great to remind students that everyone contributes to the learning that goes on, even though that might happen differently from one person to the next. In addition, there are some really good simple strategies to encourage verbal participation from a wider range of students, including more introverted students, and wait time is the first one.

Wait time is the time between when you ask a question and when you take the first response. And typically, it's a pretty short timeframe. Extending that wait time to just ten seconds, which can seem interminable, is really reflection time for the introvert. If you take a little bit longer between when you ask the question and when you take the first response, you might see more hands going up, and one of those hands might actually be of an introverted student who has had some time to think about the question before responding.

Think-ink-pair-share is another simple strategy, one that you may already be familiar with. Think-pair-share (minus the "ink") is probably the most commonly used active learning strategy in college and university classrooms across North America, and it usually goes something like this: a faculty member asks the question and says, "Think about it, then turn to your partner and share your ideas."

The extroverts in the room have turned this right away into pair-share; as soon as the faculty member asks the question, they've got something that they want to say and turn to their partners and start talking. This of course disadvantages the introverts, who would like to have a little bit more time to reflect. If you make this truly a think-ink-pair-share, it would sound something like this: "Take a minute to think about this question. Then take another minute to write down your thoughts."

If you want to let your students know that everyone contributes in class and everyone contributes differently, then having a random approach to calling on students to participate after a think-ink-pair-share really works well. I've used something called numbered heads. So, for example, if students are working in groups of four, at the end of their conversation, I would ask them to randomly count themselves off one, two, three, and four. And then I have those numbers on slips of paper that I've put into my coffee cup (without the coffee), and I ask a student to randomly pull out a number.

If the student pulls out the number two, then number twos in those small groups report back. Even introverted students who know that you're going to use this system will at least have some notice. They know that they may be called on and, given some time to prepare, are more likely to be able to respond.

Some faculty members use cold calling and use it as a way to make their students accountable, accountable for having read the material, for having prepared for class ahead of time, and for participating. I prefer to do something called *cool calling*. And cool calling is a strategy that works better for introverts because it gives them some preparation. Cool calling in my classroom might look something like this. While my students are working in groups of three or four, I wander around and eavesdrop on the conversations. And if I hear a particularly good idea, I might wander over to that student and say, "Hey, Tamika, that was a great idea. When the large group comes back together, would you be willing to participate and share your idea?"

And if Tamika is an introverted student, she has some advance notice and an invitation—she's not being called on on the spot, and she has the choice of whether to participate. Given the advanced preparation, time to think about what she said, and an invitation, even if Tamika is introverted, she may be more likely to participate.

These are just four simple strategies to encourage verbal participation in ways that help your introverted students to stretch beyond their comfort zones.

It's important to remember that difference is a good thing, and differences in our classrooms are what make classrooms rich, vibrant learning sessions. Introversion and extroversion are just one example of those kinds of differences, but if we think about respecting and celebrating differences, our classrooms become great places to be.

RECOMMENDED REFERENCE:

Monahan, N. *Helping Introverts Thrive in an Active Learning Classroom.* Magna Online Seminar. www.magnapubs.com/online-seminars/helping-introverts-thrive-in-an-active-learning-classroom-3079-1.html

Adapted from the Magna 20-Minute Mentor program, *How Do I Include Introverts in Classroom Discussion?*

Humor Increases Student Participation

Rob Kelly

Reason to read: While the study referenced focused on the use of humor in the online class, the results can be adapted to reflect any classroom setting. Humor has shown to improve the learning environment, allowing students to feel more at ease and more willing to share and participate.

The use of humor in an online course can increase students' participation, according to a recent study by Mark Shatz and Frank LoSchiavo, two Ohio University psychology professors.

The study compared two sections of the same introduction to psychology course taught by LoSchiavo. Each section used Blackboard and featured learning objectives, chapter summaries, text-based lectures, quizzes, and discussion boards. The only difference between the two sections was that one featured overtly humorous material—two or three content-relevant jokes in each of the 26 lectures, humorous cartoons in each of the 14 quizzes, and witty remarks in the course's 10 electronic announcements—and the other did not.

Although the humor in many cases was related to the content, it was not intended to enhance learning. It was intended to enhance the interest in the material and make learning more enjoyable, and that seems to have been the result. (In a future study, Shatz and LoSchiavo intend to determine the effects of humor that is designed to enhance the understanding of course content.)

"It was pretty clear that the atmosphere was different between the two sections," LoSchiavo says. "Students in the humor-enhanced section felt that everything was more casual. They spoke to me through e-mail using a somewhat different tone. They earned more class participation points, and they seemed to feel more comfortable interacting."

It's important to point out that the humor in this course was not the kind of humor that would get laughs on the comedy-club circuit or jokes that include a setup and punch line. The humor generally took the form of funny but relevant observations about the content, "something that a student might read and say, 'I can't believe my instructor wrote that.' That's what makes it funny," LoSchiavo says.

LoSchiavo established the humorous tone early in the humor-enhanced section of the course. For example, an announcement early in the course informed students that there were laptops they could borrow if they so desired. The message said, in part: "There is no charge for the laptop, but if you lose it or break it, I'll break your GPA and I might even key your car."

The course also included psychology-related cartoons with funny captions, top 10 lists (e.g., in a unit on memory: name the top 10 things you would like to forget), and jokes (e.g., in a unit on the psychology of dreaming: Martha Stewart probably dreams about trendy prison jumpsuits).

This humor (and attempted humor) acted as a social lubricant, Shatz says. "I think it's pretty similar to a traditional classroom. Once you start the course with humor, it has that snowball effect, where students become more and more comfortable. What humor does particularly well in an online environment, which can be sterile, is say, 'It's OK to communicate. It's OK to express opinions.' We don't have any hard evidence, but students' comments were also more likely to be humorous."

"You don't even have to be funny. [The students] understand you're doing it for them. When they sense your guard come down, they're more likely to interact with you," LoSchiavo says.

Based on this study and their experience incorporating humor into online courses, Shatz and LoSchiavo offer the following tips to other instructors:

- Remember that your purpose is to teach, not to make the students laugh. "A lot of instructors resist attempting humor because they don't think they're going to be funny. From our study and my professional experience, I think that students appreciate the attempt at humor. The key is to try to make it relatively low-key," Shatz says.
- Put the really funny material at the end of a unit; otherwise, students will tend to remember only the humor.
- Know your audience.
- The safest target of humor is yourself.
- Be yourself. "Humor works best when it has a personal feel," Shatz says.

- Be concise. Don't write like you're a college professor.
- Set ground rules. When you're funny, your students will also try to be funny. Without rules, some may use offensive humor.
- Have someone review your material before you post it; you may think something's funny, but others may not understand it. Humor presented live can produce a different response than when presented in print.

Humor can be used in any course, Shatz says. He has used it in his hybrid death and dying course and a statistics course. "The key is knowing when to use it," he says.

RECOMMENDED REFERENCE:

Weimer, M. "Humor in the Classroom: 40 Years of Research." *The Teaching Professor* 25(10).

Reprinted from *Online Classroom* newsletter, August 2005.

Energize Your Classroom

Alicja Rieger, PhD

Reason to read: The studies show that humor can increase motivation and enhance retention. Read on to understand where to start and how to appropriately implement humor in your own class.

Numerous studies on humor in the classroom acknowledge the important role it plays in the learning process. Humor has been reported to increase motivation, enhance the retention of new information, advance problem-solving skills, encourage creativity and critical thinking, facilitate a positive learning environment, and decrease exam anxiety (Martin, 2007). Given its importance, I'd like to suggest several ways to energize your college classroom with humor.

Use humor to get and maintain students' attention

Getting and holding students' attention every day in class is both a challenging and daunting task. Curricula are rigorous and students lead busy lives. They arrive in class after having been in other classes, having done fieldwork, or having been at work. As they sit down in overheated and crowded classrooms furnished with uncomfortable seats, even the most disciplined students may struggle to maintain attention (Skinner, 2010). But humor can help. Berk has pointed out that students cannot laugh and snore at the same time. In his 1998 book *Professors Are from Mars, Students Are from Snickers: How to Write and Deliver Humor in the Classroom and in Professional Presentations,* Berk recommends asking a series of content-related questions and following them with one or two unexpected punch-line questions. For example, suppose an education class is discussing the effectiveness of an intervention for a third-grade student with special needs. The teacher might ask this series of questions:

1. How many of you think the intervention is working for the target student?
2. How many of you think the intervention is not working for the target student?
3. How many of you think the target student owns a motorcycle?
4. How many of you would prefer to go for lunch (dinner)?

Students don't expect the last two questions. They are surprised and respond with smiles or laughter. If the teacher carries on expecting students to answer the last two questions, students become involved. They listen more attentively for answers to the important questions.

Use humor to promote critical thinking and creativity

In the college classroom, teaching should move beyond transmitting facts to encouraging students to think critically and creatively about the subject matter. According to Tamblyn (2003), students must use their imaginations and open their minds to new ideas if they are to think critically and creatively. Humor is about allowing oneself to be intellectually playful with ideas. Individuals like Albert Einstein, Thomas Edison, and Beatrix Potter have made major contributions to the world because they were persistent and mentally playful.

Simple exercises can unleash the intellectual playfulness of your students. For example, I ask my students to solve the following problem I found online: The chairs and stools in a classroom make too much noise when students sit down and get up. What can be done to achieve sweet silence? Problems like this could be created with all sorts of different content. The goal is to encourage answers outside the box.

After the exercise, ask the students the following questions: Why do we become less playful during adulthood? Why do we become less mentally playful in the academic disciplines? Why do most college professors consider play and humor adversarial to learning? Remind students that learning, if it is to be mentally playful, often entails experiencing unoriginal ideas before stumbling onto a good idea. It is said that Thomas Edison played with no less than 10,000 bad ideas before he found a right idea for the light bulb (Tamblyn, 2003).

Begin telling jokes and funny stories

Once you've gotten used to the idea of humor in your college classroom, you may consider telling jokes and/or funny stories. Here are some tips from McGhee (1994) that will increase the chances that students will respond with smiles and laughs:

- Avoid telling jokes/stories that you don't know well.
- Don't laugh at your own jokes/stories (especially before you tell them).
- Avoid starters like "This is a joke" or "I'm not very good at telling jokes, but …"
- Remember that the punch line is at the end, not somewhere else in the telling.
- Use positive humor instead of negative humor.
- Know your audience and their sensitivities. Not knowing them, you may be offensive and not even aware of it.
- Personalize or localize jokes/stories when possible.

Regardless of which approach you choose to energize your college classroom, it is essential that the humor used be directly related to the class content.

RECOMMENDED REFERENCES:

Pyrczak's (1999) *Statistics with a Sense of Humor*
Reeves' (2007) *Cartoon Corner: Humor-Based Mathematics Activities*
Paulos' (1982) *Mathematics and Humor*
Kenefick's and Young's (1993) *The Best of Nursing Humor*
Giangreco's and Ruelle's (2007) *Absurdities and Realities of Special Education: The Complete Digital Set!*

Reprinted from *The Teaching Professor* newsletter, July 2012.

Online Forum Posts Improve Discussion in a Face-to-Face Classroom

Kevin Brown, PhD

Reason to read: Online forums are not just for the online classroom anymore! The author shows us they work just as well at sparking discussion in his face-to-face classes.

Jay Howard's new book, *Discussion in the College Classroom* (a book that is well worth your time), lays out the research showing that cold calling on students is one of the best ways to get past their "civil attention." It's clear to me that once cold calling becomes the norm in a course, using that technique can increase the quality of in-class discussions.

However, most of us are loathe to use cold calling, partly because we don't like the perception it creates in students that we are out to get them, partly because we don't believe it will actually lead to a substantive answer, and partly because we believe it negatively affects our course evaluations (if we're honest). For those introverts among us who went through college courses often not talking, we also don't want to inflict expectations on students that caused us pain.

There's a middle path here, though, that I've found works quite well: online posts. I use the out-of-class posts to guide in-class discussions. In my upper-division courses, students are required to post a response to their reading by the morning of the day we'll be discussing that reading. Here are the advantages I've found with this approach.

I can use it to call on students, thereby ensuring class-wide participation. Because students have written out a comment, it's not actually cold calling. I am asking them to share something they've already thought about and prepared. I read their comments before class, and I've told them that I'll only call on them when I believe they have written something worthwhile. Knowing I value their written contribution lowers their anxiety. It also helps me because I know, more or less, what the student is going to say, and that enables me to better guide the discussion.

I can be certain that all students talk over the course of a week or two weeks or however long I want to set. They are unable to sit in class, politely pretending to listen—what Howard calls paying "civil attention." They need to be attentive because they still don't know when I'll call on them.

Their comments clarify areas of understanding or confusion. Before I walk into class, I know what I need to focus on and what I can ignore. Numerous times I've planned to elaborate on an idea only to see half the class comment on it quite intelligently in their posts. Now I simply walk into class, tell them they're on track with that idea and move us on to another discussion topic.

Similarly, I can see where students are struggling, and I now have time to spend on those parts they aren't yet understanding well. I come to discussions better prepared to handle what they're finding confusing, having had time to think through what questions I can ask or activities I can use to clarify and deepen their understanding.

Posting motivates students to do the reading. We're always looking for ways to be certain students are do the reading we've assigned. Having them write a response ahead of time ensures that they do so. This assignment is easily tweaked. Students can be assigned to add a quote from the reading that was a new insight or that raises a question for them, or they can apply an idea covered in the reading to a particular situation. It's tough to write posts responsive to prompts like these if they're only skimming the reading.

I used to give quizzes, which take up class time, but I've found that the forum posts eliminate the need for those. I've asked students who have taken different classes with me which approach they prefer, and they all say the posts. They tell me that the posts make them think more about the material and they don't feel the pressure associated with quizzes. Sometimes they have read the material but are so anxious they still miss questions.

Most students talk more on their own after I've called on them. In every class where I've taken this approach, class discussion has been more robust than in similar classes where I've used quizzes. Just two days ago, I called on a student for the first time this semester. She hadn't spoken yet, and I wanted to make sure she did. Her comment wasn't great, but it helped move the discussion in an interesting direction. Later in the class, she added a comment on her own, a phenomenon I see again and again. If

I can get students involved in the discussion in a manner that feels safe and constructive, they begin to believe they have ideas worth contributing.

For those of us who are hesitant to use cold calling, online forums offer a solid middle path. Using them encourages students to complete the assigned reading, prepare a comment about it, and that leads to much richer discussion—at least that's what's happening in my courses.

Reprinted from *The Teaching Professor* newsletter, November 2015.

Does Discussion Make a Difference?

Maryellen Weimer, PhD

Reason to read: When faced with conceptual problems, students need the opportunity to practice solving them. The value of that practice is enhanced when in addition to finding the answer, students talk to one another about the problem and how they arrived at their answers.

Here's the scenario: Students are taking a chemical thermodynamics course. The instructor solicits clicker responses to a conceptually based multiple-choice question. Students answer individually, write a brief explanation in support of their answer, and indicate how confident they are that their answer is correct. They are then encouraged to discuss their answers with two or three (self-selected) other students. After that discussion, they have the opportunity to change their answer if they wish, write another explanation for the answer, and once again indicate their degree of confidence in their answer. Do you think that discussion would make a difference—particularly, would it make a difference in their understanding of the concept?

That's the protocol students followed in the research referenced below. In one cohort, students saw how the rest of the class answered the question before their discussion, and in a second cohort they did not.

The results came down pretty substantially on the side of discussion. "A statistically significant number of students who originally had the correct multiple-choice answer had a higher value code assigned to their explanation after group discussion, and therefore demonstrated more explicit understanding of difficult concepts in chemical thermodynamics." (p. 1,482) In other words, even though they had correctly answered the question after discussing it with peers, students had a richer understanding of the answer. The same was true for students who initially answered the question incorrectly. Regardless of whether they corrected their answer or answered incorrectly again, in both cases they improved the code value of their explanations. Only when students changed a correct answer to an incorrect one did the code value of their explanations decline. However, the number of students who changed correct answers was small compared to the number who changed from incorrect to correct answers.

Whether or not students saw answer results before discussion did not seem to make a difference in whether answers were changed or in the quality of the explanations offered for the answers. Confidence in the correctness of the answer was enhanced when students saw the class response and it agreed with their answer. Likewise, when they saw the answer chosen by the majority of the class and it was not the answer they selected, their confidence diminished.

Interestingly, in this study students spent on average seven minutes in discussion. Perhaps their interactions were richer because they not only answered the question but had written an explanation supporting the answer they chose. Also of note, extra credit was awarded to students who answered correctly, which probably served to motivate participation in the discussion of answers.

This research confirms other findings reported in other research. When faced with conceptual problems, students need the opportunity to practice solving them. The value of that practice is enhanced when in addition to finding the answer, students talk to one another about the problem and how they arrived at their answers. What's most encouraging in this study is the documentation that discussion not only leads more of them to the correct answer, it improves their ability to explain why the answer is correct.

RECOMMENDED REFERENCE:

Brooks, B.J. and Koretsky, M.D. (2011). The influence of group discussion on students' responses and confidence during peer instruction. *Journal of Chemical Education, 88,* 1,477-1,484.

Reprinted from *The Teaching Professor* newsletter, April 2013.

Letting the Students Lead

Amy Getty, PhD

Reason to read: The author found out that giving the reins, and the voice, to her students opened up class discussion in amazing ways.

The joy of discussion as a class activity is starting it up and seeing where it goes. Although some of the same themes come up in every discussion, how they emerge and the connections they raise vary as much as the individual students do. On a great discussion day, the talk flows freely in interesting and unexpected directions, much like jazz.

And yet, as great as discussion is when it goes well, we've all been in class when there is no music. We start the discussion, throwing out fabulous and well-thought-out questions, which are then met with silence and blank stares, or the same five people volunteer repeatedly. And through it all, instead of talking to each other, students direct their comments to the teacher.

A few years ago, I felt that if students could wean themselves from relying on me to orchestrate class discussions, the activity would become richer and many of these problems would be solved. With this in mind, I decided to try "leading" a discussion without speaking. Although I've had to modify this original experiment, overall, I like the exercise so much it is now a regular classroom activity.

I started experimenting with my silent leadership in a children's literature class. I selected that class because I thought education majors would benefit from knowing how to lead a discussion. Previously I had students do teaching presentations and write discussion questions, but I was always there to facilitate if the discussion drifted off topic or the conversation stalled. I had never given students responsibility for leading a 30- to 45-minute discussion themselves.

At first, students were reluctant to get started. They didn't believe that

I could actually keep quiet for that long in class. I had doubts myself. But then their discussions would take off, mostly. Much to my surprise, even though I was silent, students still talked almost exclusively to me.

Each time we tried this activity, I asked students to write anonymously about their experience. After the first few trials, most felt the activity was helpful, but not perfect. Many wrote that the discussion would be better if I participated because I "knew more" than they did. Many also pointed out how anxious the activity made them feel. They looked to me for the "answers," and this decentering of the classroom made them uncomfortable.

After these initial attempts I decided to try building up to the teacher-free discussion day a bit more gradually. Since everything worth doing needs to be practiced, I began to ask students to write discussion questions from the start of the semester. We talked about which ones were effective and why. We also talked about follow-up questions and practiced improvisation. I started to incorporate students' questions into class discussion more regularly, and they started leading their own discussions in small groups.

I found that the more groundwork I incorporated at the beginning, the more successful the class-led discussions were. After I helped students build up to the teacher-free discussion, their responses also became overwhelmingly positive. Those closest to being teachers themselves valued the experience and wanted more opportunities like it. The groups even began to police themselves to make sure everyone had the opportunity to ask and answer questions. They began to talk to each other and mostly ignore me.

What started out as an experiment to garner more participation has turned into one of my favorite classroom activities. I highly recommend letting students take the lead. I believe you will find that your silence will break down theirs.

RECOMMENDED REFERENCE:

Almagno, S. "Participation Points: Making Student Engagement Visible." *Faculty Focus*. March 13, 2017.

Reprinted from *The Teaching Professor* newsletter, April 2013.

The Truly Participatory Seminar

Sarah M. Leupen and Edward H. Burtt, Jr.

Reason to read: If you have ever experienced a less-than-engaging seminar, you will want to explore the techniques the authors used to foster interactivity and participation in their upper-level seminars.

In typical upper-division seminars, each week, one student leads 10–15 classmates in a discussion of an important research paper in the field or presents his or her own work to the group. Students not presenting are supposed to participate in the discussion, but rarely do, despite professorial queries aimed at generating a lively, provocative exchange. Seminars using this format can be deadly dull. We decided to tackle the problem and would like to share our ideas for more interactive, exciting, and educationally enriched exchanges in seminars.

The most important change we made was to have every student present every week in one of three formats: one minute (approximately 7 students per week), five minutes (3–4 students per week), or fifteen minutes (two students per week). In one minute, students present an idea or introduce an organism (we teach biology) that illustrates the topic of the week. Time for questions following the one-minute presentation is unlimited. In five minutes, students are expected to present a more detailed, literature-based perspective on the topic with, again, unlimited time for questions.

The fifteen-minute category is closest to the "traditional" paper presentation on a designated topic. One week before presentation, each presenter must provide a copy of the paper or post it on the seminar website for the rest of the class and faculty. After the paper is available, every student in the seminar must post one or more open-ended questions about the paper on the seminar website at least 48 hours before the class meets. The student presenter is expected to address these questions in the presentation. After the 15 minute presentation, there is unlimited time for questions raised in the seminar. Inevitably, and delightfully, we find that the whole is greater than the sum of its parts. Without any puppet-string pulling by us, biological themes emerge from each seminar meeting. These flesh out the week's topic and unite the individual presentations.

We enforce time limits stringently using a bell to warn students when they approach the limit. When the time is up, one of us begins to ring the bell furiously thereby drowning all conversation. As soon as the student stops, we proceed to questions. We make the bell ringing something of a show, thereby adding enough levity to relax the atmosphere and provide a bit of amusement. Nonetheless, the bell does effectively end the presentation.

The format ensures that all students come prepared, that all participate in the presentations and join in the discussions that follow. We use the number of questions each student asks during the seminar as an additional measure of participation and remind students that the quality of their questions is also a factor.

Finally, instead of writing a paper read only by the instructor, each student prepares a poster for presentation at a general session on the last evening of the seminar. During the first hour of the seminar half the students stand with their posters while the instructors and half the students wander about listening to each presentation and asking questions. During the second hour the students switch roles and we repeat the process.

Throughout the semester we emphasize participation by having students post preliminary questions to a seminar website, by having students present something at every meeting of the seminar, and by having all students prepare a poster for public display and open discussion. The result is a lively seminar in which most students ask questions, pose ideas, and actively discuss controversial issues. The effect of having every student present every week is that every student is truly present every week—interested, engaged, with a "stake" in the proceedings. We and our students learn a great deal in these seminars and find that our evenings are filled with the excitement of exploring new material and finishing ahead of the bell!

RECOMMENDED REFERENCE:

Weimer, M. "Discussion Made a Difference in Student Learning." *Faculty Focus*. March 4, 2014.

Reprinted from *The Teaching Professor* newsletter, August 2008.

PART 2

•

Active Learning Strategies

Active Learning That Works: What Students Think

Kenneth Alford, PhD

Reason to read: Ken Alford got the skinny on active learning straight from his students. Here it is: exactly what students expect from, and get out of, active learning in their classes.

Over the years, I've had the opportunity to sit down with several of my students to get their feedback about learning activities. I wanted to see what students thought, just generally, about their university experience. Represented in my research were sophomores all the way through seniors, and each of them were from different majors, including the sciences, math, engineering, social sciences, film, and theater.

Engaging the senses

One of my students put it well: "It [active learning] helps you stay focused on the material that's being presented, and helps you link, make connections that you don't get from just doing the reading. The reading helps, and listening to the teacher helps. But the more senses you have engaged, whether it's sight or hearing or even smell or taste sometimes, in certain classes, it sticks better in your mind."

Learning activities allow students to put into practice, even in a little measure, what they've been learning in the classroom or reading in the book or hearing from the professor. It puts the focus back on the student and off the professor, which is, really, of course, where the focus ought to be.

The entertainment factor

Another student went on to say: "I think it's important to realize that technology and things are changing in a way that we learn differently than people did before. . . . It's hard for us to sit in a lecture, or us meaning my generation, I guess, to sit in a lecture hall and take notes on paper."

Whether the current generation actually learns differently is debatable. There have been numerous studies on that. The point here is that many of them *believe* that they learn differently. So that perception, whether true or not, means that the entertainment value needs to be increased in class. Lecture alone does not cut it, and it is hard for students today to sit in a lecture hall. Whether it be MTV or Sesame Street or whatever training they've had, students have been geared to have things constantly changing. Even movies and songs are changing in this nature. Therefore, learning activities must keep pace because these are the students that we are teaching.

Student interaction

Learning activities can give students the opportunity to interact and get to know each other. I think that's really a side benefit, but it's a wonderful benefit for them, as well as the class:

"I really enjoy when professors do give us in-class activities because it's fun to get to know your class members better. Sometimes you're in such a big lecture hall, and people are just really getting to the grind, and they lose focus that you're in a classroom of peers. And you have the opportunity to get to know them if you're presented that opportunity by a professor."

We don't want students to be spectators. The classes that you might remember from your collegiate experience are those that actually caused you to get involved. And that's the kind of setting we want to have, regardless of the topic that we're teaching.

It's important to note that learning activities can apply to any discipline. There's no discipline that's unique from wanting to engage students. The way we do it can be very, very different. But the need to engage, I think, is universal.

Collaboration

"Well, the thing about collaboration that is, I think, most valuable is just the fact that you're getting different perspectives. . . . You're getting people from different walks of life, people with different life experiences bringing new things to the subject that you're studying.

"And I think those new perspectives kind of allow you to open up your mind a little bit and be able to think a little bit more . . . instead of just what the professor is saying. It allows you to listen to other perspectives . . ."

That's one of the real benefits of learning activities. Too often students just hear my perspective and are not given time to think separately about their own views. In a learning activity, whether it's a complex learning activity such as a very involved multi-day simulation, or it's just a few minutes of a small, ad hoc group being assembled, giving students an opportunity to consider and evaluate other perspectives regarding information can be extremely valuable.

Learning activities 101: Tips to remember
- Learning activities should be the seasoning and not the main course.
- View learning activities from the student perspective.
- Understand that a new learning activity is probably not going to work perfectly the first time you introduce it.
- Learning activities should reinforce a main point.
- Allow students to practice the craft of their discipline.

An ideal learning activity allows students to explore that idea that we shouldn't define the activity space so narrowly that there's only one path to the solution. A great learning activity will give students multiple ways to reach, ideally, some of the same conclusions, and as that one did, it just gave an opportunity.

An ideal learning activity allows students to explore an idea. We shouldn't define the activity space so narrowly that there's only one path to the solution. A great learning activity will give students multiple ways to reach, ideally, some of the same conclusions.

I asked my students, "Based on what you know from previous classes you've taken, what would you tell professors that would make their class useful and beneficial for you when it comes to learning activities?" And these are some of the things they said:
- "If I had a chance to tell professors what I would like to see or improvements that I think they can make, I think the number one thing that I would tell them is that I would hope they would make it relatable to the students and show how their subject, show the strengths of their subjects and how it affects the lives of their students."
- "Advice that I would give to teachers would be to actually engage with the students. Get to know our names. Actually show excitement about the material and be willing to answer questions because when that happens, and when there's a sense of community within the classroom, that's when guards are let down, and people are able to

share really what they're feeling and questions that they have. And that's when the learning happens."

- "Just realize that students aren't going to always come to your class ready to do what you want them to do."
- "If I could tell professors what not to do, I think that that's a little harder for me to do. In general, I like to see what they do well. But I think don't make it about showing how smart you are because we know that. We respect you as professors. We respect that you know way more than we do. But drilling it into our heads through like big words and huge examples that we don't really understand doesn't really help us. And it's impressive, and like we think, wow, he's really smart. But we don't leave the classroom any better. It's an important thing to do to help the students leave feeling smarter and not feeling like, wow, my teacher is smart, but I didn't learn anything."
- "I would tell my professors to be excited about what they're teaching me. That's what really helps me the most because when my teacher is excited, I want to learn, and I want to know what they know. When they're animated in their discussions and they present it in a way that it's interesting to me, that's when it really helps me to think about it, and that's when I'm able to internalize it and make what I'm learning my own. And then I can apply it to everything."

Our goal, as faculty, is to use lecture when it's appropriate, and use learning activities when it's appropriate. And, fortunately, we're in a position, knowing the discipline, to be a better judge of that. I highly recommend that you give learning activities a shot!

RECOMMENDED REFERENCE:

Alford, K. & Sweat, A. "Getting Started with Blended Learning Videos." *The Teaching Professor 29*(10).

Adapted from the Magna Online Seminar, *Active Learning That Works: What Students Think.*

Helping Introverts Thrive in an Active Learning Classroom

Questions for Self-Reflection

For each of the following statements, indicate your response using the following options:

Agree (A) or Disagree (D)

1. I am aware of where I personally fit on the extroversion/introversion spectrum.
2. I have reflected on how my temperament might influence my preferences in teaching.
3. I provide opportunities for my students to understand their own learning preferences.
4. I am aware of the learning preferences of my students.
5. I have reviewed my participation policy in light of learning preferences.
6. I provide options to encourage all students to contribute to others' learning.
7. I consider how I use classroom time to with respect to learning preferences.
8. I provide all students with opportunities to stretch beyond their learning preferences.

Based on your response to the questions above, what next steps might you take to support both introverts and extroverts to thrive in your active learning classroom?

Next Steps: _____

_____

_____

_____

_____

_____

_____

_____

_____

_____

Active Learning Wins

Maryellen Weimer, PhD

Reason to read: Here's significant and definitive evidence that active learning really works.

For many years now, highlights from individual research studies that compare the effects of various active-learning strategies with lecture approaches have appeared in *The Teaching Professor* newsletter. Consistently, the results have favored active learning. But beyond a couple of small integrative analyses, what we've had so far is pretty much one study at a time. However, now we've got something significantly larger and more definitive.

A huge meta-analysis of the active learning-lecture research done in the science, technology, engineering, and math (STEM) fields has been completed. Its authors describe what they did. "We compared the results of experiments that documented student performance in courses with at least some active learning versus traditional lecturing by meta-analyzing 225 studies in the published and unpublished literature." (p. 8410) They actually started out with 642 studies, but with the application of five predetermined criteria (explained in the article), 225 merited inclusion in their analysis. The active-learning interventions used in the individual studies varied widely, including group problem-solving, worksheets, and tutorials completed during class; clickers; and peer instruction, among others. The amount of class time devoted to the activities also ranged widely.

The analysis focused on two related questions: 1) Does active learning boost exam scores? and 2) Does active learning lower failure rates? The answer to both questions is an emphatic yes. Deborah Allen writes in another published summary of this research, "Major findings were that student performance on exams and other assessments (such as concept inventories) was nearly half a SD (standard deviation) higher in active-learning versus lecture courses, with an effect size (standardized mean weighted difference) of 0.47." (p. 584) As for the failure rate, findings document that students in traditional lecture courses are 1.5 times more likely to fail than are students in the active-learning courses. "Average failure rates were 21.8 percent under active learning but 33.8 percent under traditional lectures—a difference that represents a 55 percent increase." (p. 8410)

As if those numbers aren't convincing enough, study authors provide additional context to make them especially significant. They report that there were 29,300 students in the 67 lecture courses analyzed in this meta-analysis. Given the failure rate data above, that means 3,516 of these students would not have failed had they been in an active-learning course.

The findings were amazingly consistent across these individual studies. There were no statistically significant differences with respect to disciplines. It didn't matter if the courses were for majors or nonmajors, lower or upper division. Although active learning had the greatest positive effect in smaller classes, the effect was positive regardless of class size.

The research team concludes, "Although traditional lecturing has dominated undergraduate instruction for most of a millennium and continues to have strong advocates, current evidence suggests that a constructivist 'ask don't tell' approach may lead to strong increases in student performance." (p. 8413)

Carl Weiman, a Nobel Prize winner in physics and now an educational research scholar, writes in a commentary on this research, "The implications of these meta-analysis results for instruction are profound, assuming they are indicative of what could be obtained if active-learning methods replaced the lecture instruction that dominates U.S. postsecondary STEM instruction." (pp. 8319–8320). He continues, "This meta-analysis makes a powerful case that any college or university that is teaching its STEM courses by traditional lectures is providing an inferior education to its students." (p. 8320)

The research team echoes these strong words by noting that if the experiments analyzed here had been randomized controlled trials of a medical intervention, they very well might have been stopped. Patients in the control condition should get the experimental treatment that was clearly more beneficial. They also argue that there is no longer any need for research that compares active learning and lectures. The lecture has been discovered to be substantially less effective. Weiman elaborates, "If a new antibiotic is being tested for effectiveness, its effectiveness at curing patients is compared with the best current antibiotics and not with treatment by blood-letting." (p. 8320)

Do note that this meta-analysis looked at research comparing active learning and lecture in the STEM fields. That's where the bulk of the empirical work is presently occurring. However, it does leave open the question as to whether active learning has the same effects in those fields on the other side of the academic house. There are individual studies indicating that it does. However, a quantitative analysis like this one has not been undertaken in other fields.

A couple of notes on references: The meta-analysis itself is not long, but the description of the statistical methods used is detailed and difficult for those without a statistical background. However, the findings are outlined and discussed clearly. In addition, Allen has written a short, understandable summary of the research and its findings, and it appears in an open access journal. It's a quick and easy way to learn more about this very important work. Weiman's commentary is also worth reading. It too offers a clear summary with easier graphics, plus insightful and pointed comments. If you ever need to make the case for active learning or have colleagues who are still unconvinced, here's the compelling evidence. Active learning wins!

RECOMMENDED REFERENCES:

Allen, D. (2014). Recent research in science teaching and learning. *Cell Biology Education—Life Sciences Education, 13* (Winter), 584-5.

Freeman, S., Eddy, S. L., McDonough, M., Smith, M. K., Okorafor, N., Jordt, H., and Wenderoth, M. P. (2014). Active learning increases student performance in science, engineering, and mathematics. *Proceedings of the National Academy of Sciences (PNAS), 111* (23), 8410-8415.

Weiman, C. E. (2014). Large-scale comparison of science teaching methods sends clear message. *Proceedings of the National Academy of Sciences (PNAS), 111* (23), 8319-8320.

Reprinted from *The Teaching Professor* newsletter, June/July 2015.

Team Teaching: Active Learning Practice for Teachers

Karen Sheriff LeVan and Marissa King

Reason to read: Change can be overwhelming. The authors have created a plan to implement team teaching in your classroom and have outlined the benefits involved in doing so, for instructors and students alike.

Most of us have applauded the various calls for a fuller understanding of active student learning, but long-term classroom change can intimidate teachers. Just like students, teachers need hands-on, feedback-filled practice to improve use of active learning in the classroom. Although team teaching is often seen as too expensive these days, the benefits of this kind of teacher collaboration are unparalleled. Team teaching takes the idea of on-the-job practice to a different level by blurring the lines between our roles as teachers and learners. Team teaching isn't a new idea, and it doesn't replace the articles, lectures, or collegial discussions we use to enlarge our instructional understandings. However, we believe it offers teachers a first-rate active learning experience because that's precisely the experience we had when we joined forces in teaching Basic Writing.

In the planning stage, before students' backpacks and personalities fill the room, professors use their own assumptions to create course structures, fashion assignments, and decide on content. Habits, rarely questioned during solitary walks from office to classroom, sometimes clash when two professors try to finalize class plans. They discover that their perspectives on the success of a class activity aren't the same, and that causes them to have a conversation during which their individual assumptions are examined. Resolution of differences often requires each team member to try new methods or refine old ones, which can feel uncomfortable but leads to professional growth. It happened that way for us. Instead of holding a new method at arms' length, we found ourselves learning from each other during planning as well as in class.

Learning to teach as you're team teaching a course is not at all like getting advice after a colleague has visited your class. In that case the decision of whether or not to follow the advice is an individual one. In team-taught courses, faculty share power, which means the switch from teacher to learner and back isn't optional; it's automatic. It forces faculty to try the new methods and learn from each other how to execute them effectively.

Even instructors who share teaching philosophies may disagree when they're evaluating an activity's success or deciding what needs to happen next in class. Team-teaching conflicts offer sustained practice that goes beyond a brief observational conversation. Learning, as our students often tell us, can be uncomfortable. Team teaching has forced us to do things we haven't done before and to learn from the experience.

Teaching-learning literature offers a robust conversation about the benefits of team teaching for students, but perhaps we need more focus on how its shared power structure so effectively transforms teachers into learners. As team teachers move separately around the room in a referee-style dance, each inevitably collects different information about what is happening in small groups or independent practice. Gathering more real-time information on student performance can clearly help students if used accurately, but what professors learn from each other needs deeper investigation. In our classrooms, we don't question each other's on-the-spot decisions, but as we teach together, we're forced to acknowledge that, like referees, we don't always see the play in the same way. With two experts in the room, it's difficult to bluff about student learning and even harder to make informed instructional decisions.

Team teaching is harder than it looks but has ongoing benefits. As we work together, we've gotten clearer about the assumptions we're making and the habits that characterize how we teach. We're also finding it easier to move our teaching styles in different directions. Though team teaching requires vulnerability to put work that feels personal in front of colleagues, it offers sustained practice that can't be had from a come-and-go peer review.

Team teaching shouldn't be ruled out automatically because of its costs. When it comes to an effective way to promote the growth and development of individual faculty members, it may be an investment more departments, programs, and institutions should consider.

In our cases, it has been one of the most memorably active learning experiences of our careers. We teach differently as a result of having taught together.

RECOMMENDED REFERENCE:

Hill, C. "Team Teaching with an Embedded Librarian." *Distance Education Report (12)*17.

Reprinted from *The Teaching Professor* newsletter, February 2015.

Incorporating Active Learning into the Online or Face-to-Face Classroom

Rob Kelly

Reason to read: Whether you teach online or face-to-face, these strategies for implementing active learning will increase interaction among your students.

Gary Ackerman, director of the Center for Teaching and Learning at Mount Wachusett Community College, works with faculty to incorporate active learning into their online and face-to-face courses, and while there are differences in these learning environments, active learning can be implemented just as well online as face-to-face.

Ackerman encourages faculty members to use the following active learning approaches in their online (as well as face-to-face) courses:

- Collaborative group work
- Writing to learn
- Questioning
- Scaffolding
- Discussion

A common element of these active learning techniques is interaction. Ackerman and several colleagues charged with leading this active-learning initiative "understand learning to be a social activity, and from our point of view, if students are not interacting with each other they're not learning," Ackerman says.

A key challenge in applying active learning to the online classroom is having to renegotiate time. For example, a discussion that might have occurred in 45 or 50 minutes in the physical classroom may take place over several weeks online in order to give everybody the time they need to reflect and have meaningful exchanges.

This asynchronous communication gives students the opportunity to revise their understanding of concepts over time as they interact with their peers. They also can review archives rather than having to rely on their memories of what was said.

The nature of the online classroom demands careful design and facilitation in order to realize the full benefits of active learning techniques. An important element of design is selecting the appropriate tools to implement the active learning techniques. In addition to the affordances of the technology, Ackerman recommends considering variety. "The literature is pretty clear that if students have the same thing over and over again they get bored with it. We have found that even simple things like using VoiceThread as an alternative for just one or two discussions makes it different enough and interesting enough so that students will pay attention in ways that they didn't previously," Ackerman says.

Discussion boards

When faculty members ask Ackerman about active learning, they tend to focus on the discussion board, and when asked about their previous experience with discussion boards, they mention a lack of focus and frequent confusion on the part of students as to who they are responding to.

"Teachers struggle understanding the differences between modeling an online discussion and an in-person one. If a [face-to-face] discussion is veering off, the instructor can nudge it back in another direction. That's difficult to do if it's online and happening over a couple of weeks, because by the time you realize it's veering off, it might be too far gone," Ackerman says. "We've been working with faculty to think really seriously and purposefully about how to begin a discussion. We think about it almost like taking a golf swing. You want to be sure to line it up right and get it on the right footing with some really good prompts."

In addition to starting a discussion with good, open-ended prompts, Ackerman recommends providing scaffolding so that students' responses are more structured and thoughtful than "I agree."

Wikis

Discussion boards are not appropriate for all interaction. For example, when an instructor asks students to list the three most important parts of the chapter, Ackerman finds that a wiki works better "because you get to see the responses evolving as a document. Everybody is seeing it. We don't have to go back and say, 'Oh yeah, that's something Sally talked about three threads ago,'" Ackerman says. Once students have provided a collective response that meets the learning objectives for that activity, the instructor can lock the wiki and then move on.

Shared documents

Ackerman recommends using shared documents as a way to engage in the active learning activity of collaborative group work. Google Docs is a good platform for collaboration. "We try to get our faculty to understand that the work of creating an online document together is not cheating. It's the type of interaction that students are going to have anyway. The question is how can we structure this interaction and make it a bit more active?" Ackerman says.

One way to make working collaboratively on a document more active is to use templates so that students have structure when they start working on the assignment, which can help prevent students from heading in the wrong direction, Ackerman says.

Blogs

Blogs can be an effective platform for discussions as well. Ackerman helped a business instructor use blogs for a case study assignment that had students look at ethical questions from several perspectives. An initial prompt presented the case and students were asked to come up with a solution. Follow-up prompts asked students to consider the case from other points of view, for example, from the perspective of a human resources professional. The blog format enabled students to clearly see a variety of perspectives on a single issue.

Synchronous chat

Due to scheduling issues, most active learning in an online course is likely to be asynchronous; however, Ackerman recommends considering synchronous activities as well. One tool that he likes is watch2gether.com, which enables students to view videos and comment on them in real time.

Recommendations for starting with active learning

Incorporating active learning techniques into any course depends on the course's learning goals as well as the instructor's teaching style and comfort level with the technology. "I see it as a continuum. ... To me, the more active learning, the better. ... I try to get faculty moving along the continuum and every little bit helps. When I work with a faculty member, I always start the conversation with, 'What's something that's brand-new in your curriculum? What's something that you don't think works very well?' Those are the places where I try to find an entry point. I try to improve those rather than having the active learning strategies be an intrusion into something that the instructor already values and that works pretty well. We look for something the instructor is uncomfortable with. Once we get that established, we hope that the next semester it's going to be something they will continue doing and maybe stretch it a little more."

RECOMMENDED REFERENCE:

Kelly, R. "Ideas for Active Online Learning." *Online Classroom*. December 2011.

Adapted from *Online Classroom* newsletter, September 2013.

Learning Assessment Techniques: How to Integrate New Activities That Gauge What and How Well Students Learn

Elizabeth Barkley, PhD

Reason to read: Barkley's model allows students to apply foundational knowledge to real-life situations, improving their engagement with and retention of the material.

A learning assessment technique (LAT) is a three-part integrated structure that helps teachers to first identify significant learning goals, then to implement effectively the kinds of learning activities that help achieve those goals, and finally—and perhaps most importantly—to analyze and report on the learning outcomes that have been achieved from those learning activities.

LATs are correlated to Fink's Taxonomy of Significant Learning, such that there are about 6–10 techniques for each of the learning dimensions, including techniques to help students learn the **foundational knowledge** of the subject and help students **apply that foundational knowledge** to real situations so that it becomes useful and much more meaningful to them. There are techniques that help students **integrate ideas**—different realms of knowledge—so that the learning is more powerful. There are techniques to help students recognize the personal and social implications of what they are learning, which is what Dee Fink calls the **human dimension**. There are techniques to help students **care** about what they are learning so that they're willing to put the effort into what they need to learn. And finally, there are techniques to help students become better and more self-directing learners (**learning how to learn**).

LATs allow you to determine how best to analyze or evaluate learning so you can actually make changes to improve student learning outcomes. Three examples you might begin with include:

- The contemporary issues journal
- Digital stories
- The personal learning environment

Contemporary issues journal

A contemporary issues journal is designed to promote learning in the **integration** dimension of the significant learning taxonomy. And that is the dimension that helps students learn how to connect different kinds of information, ideas, and experiences and to transfer these to new situations beyond their campus.

The contemporary issues journal exercise asks students to focus on the world around them to identify recent events or developments in the news that relate to their coursework. For example, they might see that information through their Facebook feeds. They might see it on their smartphones. And they are prompted to be looking constantly to see how that information relates to what they learn in class.

The contemporary issues journal can help deepen students' understanding by connecting course material to what they see in the real world. This allows students to find value in the course.

Digital stories

The digital story is designed to address the **human** dimension of Fink's learning taxonomy, which aims to help students learn more about themselves and others. The digital story allows students to use computer-based tools, such as video and audio, to share their relevant life experiences as they attempt to connect with an audience about a given issue related to the course. Though the stories can be personal or academic, they always connect course-related themes to the human experience.

Digital stories allow students to create visual representations of their personal networks for learning and provide students with a creative outlet for self-authorship and curating their lived experiences within the context of the course. They help students gain a more complete view of their own place in the world and within the course.

Personal learning environment

The personal learning environment is intended to help students achieve the **"learning how to learn"** dimension of the significant learning taxonomy, which is intended to help students continue to be independent and become more self-directed learners. The personal learning environment asks students to create a visual representation of people in their personal networks as digital resources that they can access for the specific intent of learning.

LATs are generally easy to implement structures that will help you identify learning goals, implement effective learning activities, and analyze and report on learning outcomes. Try using LATs in your class today.

RECOMMENDED REFERENCE:

Barkley, E. (2009). *Student engagement techniques: A handbook for faculty.* San Francisco, CA: Jossey Bass.

Adapted from the Magna Online Seminar, *Learning Assessment Techniques: How to Integrate New Activities That Gauge What and How Well Students Learn.*

Active Learning: Surmounting the Challenges in a Large Class

Maryellen Weimer, PhD

Reason to read: Implementing interactivity into a large class can seem daunting. Read on to see that it's not only possible, but perhaps even more effective than you might think.

"Enabling interaction in a large class seems an insurmountable task." That's the observation of a group of faculty members in the math and physics department at the University of Queensland. It's a feeling shared by many faculty committed to active learning who face classes enrolling 200 students or more. How can you get and keep students engaged in these large, often required courses that build knowledge foundations in our disciplines?

The article referenced below recounts how this faculty group did it in an introductory-level physics course required of most science majors at their university. They implemented an "integrated approach to active learning that supports the class activities with extensive preparation by both the teacher and the students. A key feature of our approach is the rich data it provides to teachers about student understanding before the start of each class." (p. 77)

Their approach has two distinct phases: what the students do before they come to class and what happens during class. As with the flipped classroom model, these students are responsible for "covering" the content before they come to class. After completing the assigned reading, students take a short online quiz that must be completed 12 hours before class. The quiz questions are conceptual and interpretative (not problem solutions), which means the answers are written out. Students get full credit if they have answered all questions "seriously" (p. 78) regardless of the number they have answered correctly. The team involved in the redesign of this course developed software that expedites the grading of the quizzes.

"Rather than the lecture being a teacher-led oration, the lecturer makes sure that any core concepts the students found difficult are discussed detail. … The focus of the class session is then a series of discussions of each of the core concepts for the lecture as defined by the learning goals for the unit of study, effectively turning the lecture into a mass tutorial experience." (p. 78) This is why the teacher needs to be able to analyze student quiz answers quickly. Those answers set the agenda for what is discussed during the class period.

In class, "each discussion starts with one or more of the students' quiz responses [that] illustrate why the concept is difficult to them. The lecturer has the students work on a series of conceptual questions designed to build and test their understanding." (p. 79) For each question, the students use clickers to answer individually, but they do not see the class response. Then they are encouraged to talk about their answer with those seated nearby, and after that they answer the question for a second time. This time they see the answers. At this point, the lecturer moves around the room with a microphone and asks students to explain why they chose a particular option, with the goal being to get multiple answers and perspectives. At the end of this exchange, the instructor reveals the right answer and summarizes the arguments that support it.

The team assessed the impact of their approach in a variety of ways. Physics is one of those fields that has developed standardized tests that can be used to measure knowledge before and after a first course. Two of these tests were used to measure learning gains in this study. For the Force Concept Inventory, the normalized gain for 154 students (in one course section) was 58 percent. Other research has established that the normalized gain in the same course taught in more traditional ways is 23 percent. In the second section, using the Brief Electricity and Magnetism Assessment, the normalized gain was 47 percent, which can be compared with 23 percent in traditional first-year university classes. Those are impressive gains.

The team also considered the effects of student engagement as measured by the clicker responses. The average percentage of correct answers when students responded individually was 55 percent. It jumped to 67 percent after students interacted with each other. A series of focus group interviews with students revealed an overall favorable response to the course design. The students noted how valuable it was when the majority of the class chose the incorrect answer to one of the conceptual questions, especially when they were confident they had answered it correctly. When they discovered they were wrong, as one student observed, "That's when I learn the most. That is revolutionary." (p. 83) The standard course evaluation surveys also confirmed the positive response to this course redesign. "Our first unit was ranked among the highest first-year science courses for both overall student satisfaction, and for the amount of 'helpful feedback' received by students." (p. 84)

The article continues with a discussion of faculty experiences preparing for and teaching the course. "It's a completely different activity when you walk into the room knowing exactly where students are in their own words—in a normal class you often don't find out until you make the final exam!" (p. 84) Teachers arrive in class knowing what students don't understand, what they misunderstand, and what is causing confusion. That said, the teachers in this project found that the approach required more preparation time. Some of this involved first-time-through issues such as the generation of the conceptual questions used on the quizzes and in class. These could be reused, refined, or revised in subsequent classes. As might be suspected, it was also challenging for those faculty who were used to lecturing to talk less, giving students the time they needed to think and talk about the content.

"We cannot identify a single aspect of our approach that works above all others; it is the integration of all the practices into a coherent process that makes it such a powerful teaching and learning intervention." (p. 86)

This article is noteworthy for another reason. It's the whole package—what exactly the faculty implemented (with references that support their design features), how they assessed the changes, what their results showed, and what they learned through the process. It's a remarkable piece of scholarship—it's both useful and readable!

Reference: Drinkwater, M. J., Gannaway, D., Sheppard, K., Davis, M. J., Wegener, M. J., Bowen, W. P., and Corney, J. F. (2014). Managing active learning processes in large first-year physics classes: The advantages of an integrated approach. *Teaching and Learning Inquiry: The ISSOTL Journal, 2* (2), 75-90.

RECOMMENDED REFERENCE:

Weimer, M. "Active-Learning Ideas for Large Classes: Simple to Complex." *The Teaching Professor 25*(3).

Reprinted from *The Teaching Professor* newsletter, April 2015.

Reflecting on Active Learning Experiences 30 Years Ago

Bonnie Farley-Lucas, PhD

Reason to read: Looking back on 30 years of active learning activities gives great perspective on how active learning can stand out to students and shape their education throughout their lives.

As part of a keynote panel discussion for the Improving University Teaching Conference in Santiago, Chile (July 2013), I was asked to ponder the issue of "30 Years of Active Learning." Active learning has a much longer history than that, but I have had 30 years to reflect on, and benefit from, my active learning experiences in college.

I started college in 1983. I can recall a few impressive lectures from passionate professors, but most of the content-based learning has evaporated from memory. What stands out after all those years are the active learning experiences that led me to retain certain nuggets of knowledge and helped me grow as a person. Here are six critical learning experiences I had in college that shaped my knowledge and, ultimately, my career choices.

1. Interview-based assignments. Through interview-based assignments, I practiced valuable skills and learned empathy and respect for diversity. For a cross-cultural communication class, I interviewed an Australian student who opened my eyes to cultural preferences and similarities rather than differences. From an interview with a university administrator I learned of the many career possibilities in higher education.

2. Team-based assignments. Assignments that involved using cases, role-plays, and simulations taught me problem solving and group communication. They also allowed me to test my participation and leadership skills.

3. Independent research projects with an interdisciplinary connection. Projects that allowed me to pursue my own interests and delve deeper into a subject area were both enjoyable and memorable. I still have clear memories of several research projects, one that explored the portrayal of children in medieval portraits, another visual project on market supply and demand, and a project for which I created a human resources database. I left college liking research and thinking of it as a puzzle to be solved.

4. Out-of-class communication with professors. Several caring professors provided positive feedback and encouraged me to explore their disciplines. For example, Dr. Jane Hamilton Merritt, a Pulitzer Prize–nominated journalist who spent time in a Buddhist temple, chronicled the Hmong people of Laos and brought the Vietnam War into our living rooms. She taught me to appreciate the writing of Pearl Buck and other world travelers who just happened to be women. She created in me the desire to travel the world.

5. Participation in campus organizations and events. When I was a new student, campus clubs and organizations gave me a sense of belonging and allowed me to meet others. Later, as a leader of campus organizations, I acquired more valuable interpersonal skills and learned to work with those at different levels in the campus community.

6. Internships. An internship at a New York advertising agency taught me about organizational functioning and gave me the opportunity to practice professionalism. It also provided the backdrop for another key learning experience, writing an honors thesis on organizational development. Together, these two active learning experiences led me to pursue a master's degree in organizational development, launched my first career as a communication trainer and consultant, and ultimately led me to earn a PhD in communication.

Thirty years after these college experiences, I am a communication professor and director of faculty development who employs and advocates student engagement in teaching and learning. Active learning experiences and high-impact practices, including team-based learning, problem-based learning, interdisciplinary connections, independent research, and internships, helped me thrive as a student. The added values of faculty-student interaction outside class and campus involvement led not just to better learning, but also to more career opportunities. I am grateful for the many excellent professors who cared enough to structure these life-changing learning experiences. If after 30 years any of my students remember an active learning experience that happened in one of my classes, I would consider that a teaching success. I would also be grateful and honored.

RECOMMENDED REFERENCE:

Weimer, M. "Active Learning: Endorsed but Not Used." *The Teaching Professor 29*(3).

Reprinted from *The Teaching Professor*, January 2014.

Should I Encourage Experiential Learning?

Barbara Jacoby, PhD

Reason to read: Experiential learning can be effective for students of varying learning styles and allows students to take ownership of their learning. The author defines experiential learning and gives useful examples to apply in your own classes.

I recently came across a study that showed that 40 percent of students in college lectures are focusing on something other than what the faculty member is talking about. Lectures are sometimes just simply not engaging. We also know from studies like *Academically Adrift* that students are graduating without acquiring critical skills, particularly in the areas of thinking, reflection, creative problem-solving, and collaborative work. These are the kinds of skills that students can gain through experiential learning inside and outside the classroom.

Learning does not happen if students are not challenged and engaged, and boredom can be a problem. Let us look at what is and is not experiential learning, when to use it inside the classroom, examples of activities that you can do in class, and steps for design and implementation.

What is experiential learning?

Experiential learning is a process through which a learner constructs knowledge, skill, and value from direct experience—it's learning-centered. The faculty member is the guide on the side, not the sage on the stage, and it's not about "chalk and talk," as one of my colleagues calls the lecture method. We guide students through the process of learning.

The nature of the teaching experience really changes from transferring knowledge to be regurgitated on an exam to guiding students through the process of learning while we provide information and resources, and we actually have the opportunity to watch them learn. As faculty members, our role is to select those learning experiences, pose problems, and work with our students to co-create a learning environment that's safe. We support students as learners and facilitate critical reflection.

Experiential learning is not about transfer of knowledge to be regurgitated, or "students teaching themselves," which is what I sometimes hear colleagues say when they don't really get it. It's certainly not lightweight, fluffy, or busywork. It is not about experience alone because experience is not always the best teacher when it happens without critical reflection. It's not only for narrowly defined professional training. And it's certainly not something that happens only outside the classroom.

Why use experiential learning inside the classroom?

Experiential learning allows instructors to immediately correct mistakes. We can correct misconceptions or misapplication of data in the moment rather than waiting to see it come back to us on homework or exams, which really frustrates everyone. It's well suited for those students with busy schedules—be it a heavy academic course load, work or family responsibilities, or a combination of the two—who just simply may not have time to take on one more activity outside the classroom.

Experiential learning also is good for students with varying learning styles, and so it's great for those who can learn best through concrete active learning experiences as well as those who like to think abstractly and then apply. It also teaches students to work and learn collaboratively as they will in the workplace. It works very well in large classes, and I'll show you that as we go along. Faculty can observe students in practice for direct assessment, and it's easier to organize and control than out-of-class activities.

You can use experiential learning to address learning outcomes that involve the synthesis and analysis of information to be used in solving complex problems and applying concepts to practice in a new context. For example, calculus isn't and shouldn't be just the ability to run through calculations to get an answer. But it's much richer and certainly much more effective for students to understand and apply its concepts to new problems.

Experiential learning is great for effective communication in oral, written, and other forms of communication and media, and also for working collaboratively. It enables students to exercise well-reasoned judgment. It's great for taking ownership of learning, for learning how to learn. It's also effective for students to get to use a discipline's knowledge base to address social issues—the application of knowledge. And it's useful for other outcomes that involve things like relating, interpreting, prioritizing, and decision-making.

I wouldn't necessarily suggest using experiential learning for outcomes that involve the transfer of knowledge, memorization of data, identifying, ordering, checking things, or when there's only one correct answer. Without any doubt, experiential learning inside the classroom can take many forms. Let's look at some real examples, and then we'll get into the actual steps of implementation.

Simulations

Simulations, particularly role-play, are a favorite of mine. In role-play, students are given a situation that contains two or more different perspectives or viewpoints. The students usually receive a prepared brief that provides the different perspectives on the same situation. The different perspectives are given to different students, who then take on the role of that perspective. The students then come together and work through the situation.

This is how it works well in large classes: You can have one group of students enacting a role-play in front of a large lecture hall, and then the other students can reflect in small groups about what they saw and provide feedback. Or if your classroom allows, you could have varying groups of students doing role-plays in different corners of the classroom.

Problem-based learning

Problem-based learning is the more challenging cousin of a case study, which is the preferred method of learning in law school classes. In working with a case study, students get all the facts and sometimes the end result or the solution to analyze. However, in problem-based learning, students are engaged in solving complex, multifaceted real or realistic problems that can be solved in different ways and may have more than one solution, so students really get involved.

Students work inside the class in groups, under the guidance of the faculty member. Groups can each address the same problem and then come together to share their solutions. Or they can have the same problem but use parallel processing so that each student group addresses a different facet of the problem, then come together, put the facets together, and seek out the optimal solution.

In the process of problem-based learning, students identify what they know that applies to the situation, what else they need to know, and how they will acquire high-quality information that will enable them to reach what they feel is the best conclusion. In the process, students also often deliberate and resolve any ethical issues that exist in the kernel of the problem.

Group projects

Students may roll their eyes at *another group project*. Well, it's different when you do it inside the classroom, and I'll tell you why. In professional settings, individuals work together in teams on complex, multifaceted tasks. Group projects allow students to do projects inside the classroom for real or hypothetical businesses or nonprofits.

Debate and deliberation

Debate, as we know, is oppositional. The debaters seek to win. They submit their beliefs, their best thinking, and their conclusions, trying to capitalize on the opponent's weaknesses to win the debate. Deliberation is a collaborative process, one in which we seek each other's strengths. We seek the best solutions, and generally, we're seeking common ground for common action.

Debate and deliberation on controversial issues that come up in every single discipline is a powerful method of learning. A few sample topics across disciplines include stem cell research, universal health care, censorship in the Internet, the environment, gun control, and immigration law. If appropriate, students can put into civic action the conclusions from their debate or deliberation by writing a letter to the editor of an influential local or national publication, preparing real or mock testimony on the issue, and the like.

Critical reflection

Critical reflection and experiential learning engage students in thinking about and answering questions like these: What did I learn? Where did that information come from? How reliable is this information? What does it mean for me? What questions remain? How will I use my knowledge in the future? Critical reflection and experiential learning can take many forms: individual or group and through oral, written, or other media.

Experiential learning engages students intellectually, socially, and emotionally so that their learning feels authentic. They have the confidence to use it in the future. One of the great joys of experiential learning inside the classroom is we have the opportunity to create those situations, guide students through them, and watch them learn. I hope you will give it a try.

RECOMMENDED REFERENCES:

Austin, J. & Raffo, D. (2009). "Make it happen: Developing and implementing experiential learning programs." *Academic Leader (25)*7.

Jacoby, B. *Experiential Learning Inside the Classroom.* Magna Online Seminar. www.magnapubs.com/online-seminars/experiential-learning-inside-the-classroom-3057-1.html

Adapted from the Magna 20-Minute Mentor presentation, *Should I Encourage Experiential Learning in Class? How?*

Levels of Critical Reflection

Barbara Jacoby, PhD

Level One	Example
• Gives examples of observed behaviors or characteristics of the client or setting, but provides no insight into reasons behind the observation; observations tend to be one dimensional and conventional or unassimilated repetitions of what has been heard in class or from peers. • Tends to focus on just one aspect of the situation. • Uses unsupported personal beliefs frequently as "hard" evidence. • May acknowledge differences of perspective but does not discriminate effectively among them.	"My tutee told me she couldn't do her homework last night, that it was too noisy to work in her apartment and that there was no place to do it. I don't understand why her parents don't care about her education. I know they have only recently come to the U.S. from Central America, but...."

Level Two	Example
• Observations are fairly thorough and nuanced although they tend not to be placed in a broader context.	"I saw for myself that the areas where Black people lived are still in worse than the areas where there are mostly white people. It's not just that the Black neighborhoods seemed to be more severely damaged, but also that help is coming much more slowly. Is this racism or have the people in the white neighborhoods been more persistent about getting help?"
• Provides a cogent critique from one perspective, but fails to see the broader system in which the aspect is embedded and other factors which may make change difficult.	
• Uses unsupported personal beliefs and evidence but is beginning to be able to differentiate between them.	
• Perceives legitimate differences of viewpoint.	
• Demonstrates a beginning ability to interpret evidence.	

Level Three	Example
• Views things from multiple perspectives; able to observe multiple aspects of a situation and place them in context. • Perceives conflicting goals within and among the individuals involved in a situation and recognizes that the differences can be evaluated. • Recognizes that actions must be situationally dependent and understands many of the factors that affect their choice. • Makes appropriate judgments based on reasoning and evidence. • Has a reasonable assessment of the importance of the decisions facing people and of his or her responsibility as a part of other people's lives.	"When we got to Panama, the people we met had mixed reactions to us. They said that they had had other groups of volunteers come for a week at a time and that they enjoyed talking with us, even if it was kind of difficult across the language barrier. We told them we were there because it was our spring break, and we were there to educate the women about sanitation, disease prevention, and nutrition. They were interested, but it was hard for them to come to our programs because it was harvest time. I wonder if we came at our convenience or theirs. They also already had some education about some of the topics by other groups. Perhaps we should be helping with the harvest now and come back at another time for the education part. I also wonder if we should ask them what topics they most want to learn about before we come next time."

Adapted from Bradley, J. (1995). "A model for evaluating student learning in academically based service." In Troppe, M., *Connecting cognition and action: Evaluation of student performance in service learning courses.* Providence, RI: Campus Compact.

The Success of Four Activities Designed to Engage Students

David Burrows, PhD

Reason to read: The author not only implemented four active learning techniques into his classes, but then analyzed the effectiveness of each of them.

How can we engage students who are enrolled in large courses so they become active learners? I used four activities designed to get students involved, support their efforts to learn, and personalize the material in an introductory psychology course. How well did they work? For analysis, I divided the 52 students in my course into four groups, or quadrants, using their final overall course scores to place them in high- to low-performance groups. Final course scores were computed as points on a scale of 1 to 100, which were then reported as letter grades. Then I looked at how involved students in each group were in the engagement activities. I'll start with a description of each of the engagement activities.

Optional retake exams. There were three in-class exams (each worth 20 percent) and a final exam. Each exam included short-answer and essay questions. Students could opt to retake any or all of the three in-class exams. The retakes, administered electronically, were personalized. For questions that students missed on the exam, new versions of the questions appeared on their individually constructed retake exam. Retakes were therefore a mastery system that encouraged students to focus on those concepts they did not understand. Based on the retake scores, points were added, not subtracted.

Self-designed essays. Before every exam, each student had the option of submitting an essay question that then became one of the questions on her or his exam. This gave students a chance to focus on a question, hopefully one of interest to them, and prepare an answer in advance of the exam.

In-class writing. The course included 10 "two-minute write" exercises, done in class. These focused on understanding key concepts or applying course material to real-life situations. For example, "Provide an example of how understanding the nervous system can improve the quality of psychological life." For each in-class write completed, students earned one point on their final course score, up to a maximum of seven points.

Optional review sessions. These were scheduled before each exam during non-class times. Students were asked to bring questions to these sessions.

Students could also test their knowledge of key concepts in advance of exams using a self-rating system. In class, we debated controversial topics using student teams.

Here's a brief summary of how well each of these approaches engaged students in learning the course content.

Optional retake exams. The percentage of retakes (starting with those in the highest quadrant, moving to the lowest) were 12 percent, 51 percent, 44 percent, and 51 percent. The average improvement in each test score for the four groups was, respectively, 4.42, 4.55, 6.76, and 10.3 percentage points. Estimates of the improvement in the final course percentage for anyone taking all three retakes were 2.65, 2.73, 4.06, and 6.18 (again from the highest to the lowest group). The potential grade enhancements ranged from one-quarter of a final letter grade for the strongest students to more than one-half a letter grade for the lowest-performing students. Overall, students took 38 percent of the maximum number of retake exams. Students in the lowest-scoring group did not do retakes that would have substantially improved their course grades.

Self-designed essays. The total number of questions submitted by students in the highest to lowest groups were 17, 13, nine, and one. Overall, the percentage of submitted questions was 25 percent of the maximum possible, with a badly skewed distribution. The lowest-performing students took virtually no advantage of this opportunity, submitting one essay out of a potential for 39 submissions.

In-class writes. The average number of completed writes by quartile of student success was 9.43, 9.38, 9.77, and 7.15 (again, highest to lowest). In addition to showing lower participation, 39 percent of the bottom-quadrant students completed fewer than the minimum required number of seven.

Optional review sessions. There were four review sessions, one before each in-class examination and one before the final. The percentages of sessions attended by students in the four success quadrants were 30 percent, 33 percent, 41 percent, and 31 percent (highest to lowest). It is notable that students in the lowest quadrant were no more likely to attend such sessions than the other students were.

As a whole, students took substantial but not universal advantage of these activities. Students in the lowest quadrant passed up many opportunities to improve their scores. Students in the lowest-performing group took 51 percent of the maximum possible exam retakes, 2.6 percent of the maximum opportunities to write an essay question, 72 percent of the maximum possible in-class writing opportunities, and 31 percent of possible exam review opportunities. Their choices seem to reflect a lack of engagement, motivation, or perhaps self-confidence. What I learned from this endeavor is if we simply provide engagement activities and opportunities, we cannot assume that those who need them most will take advantage of what's being offered.

RECOMMENDED REFERENCE:

Cassidy, A. *Student Engagement Four-Pack.* Magna Online Seminars. www.magnapubs.com/online/mentor/student-engagement-4-pack-3101-1.html

Reprinted from *The Teaching Professor* newsletter, October 2015.

Active Learning: A Perspective from Cognitive Psychology

Suzanne M. Swiderski, PhD

Reason to read: Becoming familiar with the cognitive psychology background of active learning will allow you to better recognize the process through which students learn, allowing you to incorporate active learning strategies that promote cognitively oriented understanding.

In recent years, the phrase "active learning" has become commonplace across the academic disciplines of higher education. Indeed, most faculty members are familiar with definitions that go something like this: Active learning involves tasks that require students not only to do something, but also to think about what they have done. Moreover, many faculty have already incorporated into their teaching activities associated with active learning, such as interactive lectures, collaborative learning groups, and discussion-related writing tasks.

However, faculty may not be aware that, from the perspective of cognitive psychology, the meaning of active learning is slightly different. According to cognitive psychology, active learning involves the development of cognition, which is achieved by acquiring "organized knowledge structures" and "strategies for remembering, understanding, and solving problems." (This particular definition is from a cognitive psychology text edited by Bransford, Brown, & Cocking, *How People Learn: Brain, Mind, Experience, School.*) Additionally, active learning entails a process of interpretation, whereby new knowledge is related to prior knowledge and stored in a manner that emphasizes the elaborated meaning of these relationships.

Faculty interested in promoting this cognitively oriented understanding of active learning can do so by familiarizing their students with such cognitive active learning strategies as activating prior knowledge, chunking, and practicing metacognitive awareness.

- **Activating prior knowledge**
  Students need to determine what they already know about a particular principle so any preconceptions or misconceptions can be corrected before further learning occurs. For example, prior to teaching about the process of photosynthesis, a biology instructor could discuss with students their current understanding of the ways plants gain nutrition. By doing so, the instructor can correct any erroneous information so that students are not attempting to reconcile misinformation with the appropriate information the instructor will shortly present.

- **Chunking**
  Students need to be able to group individual pieces of information into larger, more meaningful units, so these "chunks" of information can be remembered and retrieved in an efficient manner. A mathematics instructor, for instance, could help students learn by presenting strategies used to solve problems as groups of integrated steps, with meaningful connections between these steps, rather than as isolated tactics that could be combined in several different ways.

- **Practicing metacognitive awareness**
  Students need information about their own thinking processes so they can effectively plan, monitor, and evaluate their progress in learning. For example, while teaching a specific Greek epic, a classics instructor could discuss with students where in the text they experienced difficulty and how they resolved that difficulty. By doing so, the instructor encourages students to reflect on the comprehension strategies that they are already using, as well as to learn other useful strategies from their peers.

Faculty interested in promoting active learning should not attempt to incorporate all of these cognitive active learning strategies into their instruction in a single period, or even during a single week, because doing so would likely prove overwhelming to students. Rather, they might consider choosing a single strategy, teaching it to students, and then repeatedly requiring the use of it—for in- and out-of-class tasks—throughout a semester. If they provide students with instruction in the strategy and follow that instruction with opportunities for practice and feedback, they will help students make the strategy a natural and automatic part of their learning efforts.

Reference: Bransford, J. D., Brown, A. L., and Cocking, R. R. (Eds.) 2000. *How people learn: Brain, mind, experience, school.* Washington, D.C.: National Academy Press.

RECOMMENDED REFERENCE:

Price, C. *How Can I Create Effective Mini-lectures?* Magna 20-Minute Mentor Presentation. www.magnapubs.com/online/mentor/how-can-i-create-effective-mini-lectures-3170-1.html

Reprinted from *The Teaching Professor*, March 2007.

Active Learning: Informal Writing Assignments Rubric

Scott Warnock, PhD

First, what do you want the assignment to accomplish?
- Your answer should be based specifically on course/unit/class goals.
- You need a clear view of these goals to create a useful/usable rubric.

Decide on simple, straightforward areas to assess.
- One or two clear criteria could be enough for a rubric that helps you evaluate informal writing assignments.
- Again, make sure the criteria are integral to the overall assignment goals.
- In many cases, these criteria should be content-oriented and very specific. For example, a short response to a reading could have these two criteria:

  1. Demonstrate understanding of the chapter (1 to 5 scale)?
  2. Quality of writing (1 to 5 scale) (judged loosely, maybe your readerly response: Did you not understand part of this because of writing mechanics?).

- A key question is this: What don't you want to worry about? You don't want to assess everything, or you'll end up getting frustrated with the use of rubrics—and the use of informal writing.
- Participation, length aren't great criteria, but they're something you can work with for a short assignment.

Decide on a number of performance levels for your criteria.
- Develop four or five levels of performance.
- Use simple, clear language: E.g., Excellent, Good, Fair, Poor, Unacceptable.

Decide how you want to respond to a range of student responses.
- This part can be tricky.
- What do you say to the student who has performed best for a given criterion? What do you say to the student who has done poorly?
- Again, the language in your rubric responses should be clear—and this will help you think about the way you are envisioning the assignment in the context of their learning.

A Quiz That Promotes Discussion and Active Learning in Large Classes

Patricia L. Stan, PhD

Reason to read: Getting students to think about and apply course concepts is the name of the game. This author's take-home quiz activity has shown to do just that.

Educational research is full of studies that show today's students learn more in an active-learning environment than in a traditional lecture. And as more teachers move toward introductory classes that feature active-learning environments, test performance is improving, as is interest in these classes. The challenge for teachers is finding and developing those effective active-learning strategies. Here's a take-home quiz activity that I've adapted and am using to get students interested in my course content.

I teach a large, non-major chemistry course. I try to include topics such as pollution sources, alternative fuels, nutrition videos, and hometown water supplies that are relevant to students in different majors. I give a five-question quiz assignment several days before the topic comes up in class and then use it to facilitate class discussion. I want students thinking and applying course content. The first thing I ask for is a link to a recent article or video of interest to the student within the designated topic area (e.g., Find a recent article that describes an alternative energy source). Question two asks for a general understanding or definition (e.g., Is this energy source renewable or nonrenewable? Explain.). Next are questions that encourage students to interpret what they've read and assess its reliability (e.g., How does this energy source compare to oil and coal? Or how will this energy source help meet our current and future energy needs?). The quiz wraps up with a question that asks for the student's opinion on the topic (e.g., Burning garbage to produce electricity is an alternative fuel—would you be happy to see your town adopt this method? Explain.).

Elements in this assignment connect with the documented learning needs of millennial students. The quiz covers topics that are current and relevant. It asks for a personal application. Students use technology; they insert a link to the article and look it up/turn it in online. I stipulate news sources, no blogs or Web pages, so that they learn to be discerning in their use of the technology. Their opinions matter, and they are asked to express them. Last, they are rewarded for work—as long as they put forth reasonable effort, they get full credit.

The activity also fits with my teaching priorities. It's an assignment that prepares students to actively participate in our discussion of the topic. I can call on anyone without putting him or her on the spot. I scan their answers ahead of time, which allows me to highlight points related to my learning outcomes. The questions push students to engage with the material on a deeper level. They are encouraged to use logic and science to support their opinions. As we discuss, I can share my interpretation and ask for theirs. We deal with topics on which beliefs and opinions differ. During these exchanges students are challenged to be critical of what they read. Their growing knowledge of science helps them better support their beliefs and propose wiser decisions. And I can explain that science is not always right. As scientists learn more, what we believe and the actions we propose change as well.

Being able to pick topics of interest motivates students. Our discussions are informal and lively. I have found this approach reduces the fear of giving a wrong answer in front of the class, so more students participate. These discussions help me understand how those outside chemistry view it. I look forward to these discussions because I get to know students, and they get to see how a scientist thinks. Sometimes they are surprised to learn that we don't have all the answers.

After a take-home quiz discussion, I often get emails from students with more article links related to our discussions. The formula for this activity isn't new—have students look something up, apply it to their lives, and express their opinions. However, I've discovered that using it as a quiz effectively prepares and motivates students for class discussions of the topic.

RECOMMENDED REFERENCE:

Weimer, M. "An Innovative Quiz Strategy." *The Teaching Professor* (25)7.

Reprinted from *The Teaching Professor* newsletter, March 2015.

Quick Feedback, Engaged Students

Kevin Brown, PhD

Reason to read: Most instructors agree that feedback is key to keeping students on track. Here are some actionable strategies to providing engaging feedback efficiently.

We often wonder what we can do to help students engage with the material so they can learn it at a deeper level. Students don't make that an easy task. They arrive in class having not read the material or having not thought about it in meaningful ways, and that keeps them from being engaged in class. Several years ago, I read George Kuh's article "What Student Engagement Data Tell Us about College Readiness," in which he writes, "Students who talk about substantive matters with faculty and peers are challenged to perform at high levels, and *receive frequent feedback* on their performance typically get better grades, are more satisfied with college, and are more likely to persist" (*Peer Review*, January 1, 2007, p. 4; italics mine). Here are three ways I try to provide feedback that engages students and not overwhelm myself with grading tasks in the process.

Short essays

Whenever I mention essays to colleagues, they worry that I am suggesting they spend every weekend reading papers. I have found two shorter assignments that help students and me know if they are understanding the material and that can be graded quickly. The note-card essay limits student responses to a 3x5 or 4x6 card. One of my colleagues has his upper-level students create a question and then write a response to it. He uses the questions and answers on their cards to stimulate discussion in class. He finds that doing so draws out students who don't often speak in class.

Also, I use one-page essays that focus on a single skill or idea, a technique I stole from Irvin Hashimoto's *Thirteen Weeks*. In my freshman composition course, I assign several of these essays, but I grade them only for thesis and evidence (or whatever skill I'm having students practice). In a sophomore literature survey, they focus on one idea, such as reason or passion in *The Enlightenment*. Even in junior-level literature courses, the students respond to a quote from a critic, giving them practice at integrating and responding to quotations in their writing. Doing so helps them avoid the random sprinkling of quotations throughout their longer papers.

Online forums

Most college and university computer systems include some sort of forum or blog capability. We use Moodle, where I can set up a forum for students to post and respond. In my upper-division courses, students post 150- to 250-word responses to the assigned readings. These responses are long enough to encourage interaction with the text but not so long that it takes me more than 20 to 30 minutes to read an entire class's responses. Like my colleague, I use their responses to provoke class discussion. Having written a response, most students come to that discussion with an idea already in mind. This encourages those reluctant to participate to offer ideas and insights.

These online forums have other benefits as well. First, I do not have to spend class time on ideas students already understand. Since I read their posts before class, I can see that 15 or 20 of them have all commented on an idea I had planned to discuss. When it's clear they understand the idea, I mention it briefly in class, praising them for recognizing its importance, and then I move on to some idea not discussed in their posts. If their responses contain evidence that they are confused about or misunderstanding an idea, I can address that in class. When I mention that several posts indicated confusion about an issue, students see that they weren't the only ones not understanding something in the reading. Sometimes I intervene in the forum, offering clarification, but I still spend time on the idea in class to make sure it is clear.

Process writing

We tend to talk about the writing process only in freshman composition courses. However, using the process in all disciplines—where students sequentially turn in an annotated bibliography and rough draft, go through peer editing and conferences with professors, and then turn in a final draft—gives them consistent feedback throughout the process. They produce better papers as a result. You can help them deepen their thinking as they work on the paper. You can catch writing and bibliography problems and can raise questions about content that may be plagiarized. Talking with students about their topics and reading bibliographies is not time consuming, and taking such steps makes the writing process a richer learning experience. If they submit better papers, that speeds up the grading process at the end of the course.

Students are more likely to be engaged in classes when they receive regular feedback. It keeps them on track. Shorter assignments, technology, and process writing can help engage students, leading to better discussion and more complex thinking, and those results benefit students and teachers.

Reprinted from *The Teaching Professor* newsletter, November 2012.

Three Active Learning Strategies That Push Students Beyond Memorization

Sydney Fulbright, PhD

Reason to read: If improving retention of information is one of your goals as an instructor, try the following strategies to move your students from passive to active learning, improving retention and making class more fun in the process.

Those who teach in the health disciplines expect their students to retain and apply every iota of learned material. However, many students come to us having achieved academic success by memorizing the content, regurgitating that information onto an exam, and promptly forgetting a good portion of it. In health, as well as other disciplines where new material builds upon the material from the previous semesters, it is critical for students to retain what they learn throughout their coursework and as they begin their careers as a nurse, engineer, elementary teacher, etc.

So, how do we get students to retain this knowledge? Here are three active learning strategies for pushing students beyond simple memorization.

Case studies and simulations

Forsgren, Christensen, and Hedemalm (2014) found that case studies stimulate the student's own thinking and reflection, both individually and in groups. Through reflection, the student gains a broader view, increased understanding, knowledge, and deeper learning. Case studies are a form of problem-based learning that encourage the student to think critically and apply "book knowledge" to everyday practice and problems that will occur in the workplace. A literature review reveals very little research on using case studies in fields other than health, law, and business. However, case studies could certainly be written for any field of study.

Many other methods of assisting with knowledge retention come from healthcare fields but can easily be adapted to other majors. Simulation— whether high-tech as in mannequins or low-tech as in role play—is a good method to help the student apply knowledge to real world scenarios.

Concept maps

Concept maps are graphical tools for organizing and representing knowledge and can be used to help students visualize connections between words and concepts. The first step is defining a focus question or problem which the student then internalizes a strategy for defining and clarifying (Eberly Center for Teaching Excellence, 2014). Concept maps using real world situations can help reinforce key ideas by encouraging students to think both creatively and analytically about previously learned information and apply it to new scenarios.

One-minute papers

A classic among active learning techniques, the one-minute paper remains a simple yet effective way to gauge student learning. I use these papers as an assessment of my own teaching efficacy but more importantly to get students to reflect on what went on in the classroom that day. My questions are all open-ended so as to encourage reflection and feedback on the subject matter.

Possible prompts for a one-minute paper, include:
- The clearest point of today's class was:
- The muddiest point of today's class (or something that confused me or I want clarified) was:
- How I prepared for class today:
- What I liked best that helped me learn:
- What I wish had been discussed during today's class:

In summary, we all know that lecturing is not the most effective manner of teaching, any more than cramming is an effective form of learning. Active learning strategies such as these move students from passive to active participation in their learning; boosting retention in the process. As an added bonus, these methods fit well in the flipped learning environment that many instructors are using today.

RECOMMENDED REFERENCES:

Eberly Center for Teaching Excellence. *Whys and hows of assessment.* Carnegie Mellon. http://www.cmu.edu/teaching/assessment/howto/ assesslearning/conceptmaps.html

Forsgren, S., Christensen, T., & Hedemalm, A. (2014). Evaluation of the case method in nursing education. *Nurse Education in Practice.* 14, 164–169.

Reprinted from *Faculty Focus*, July 9, 2014.

PART 3

•

Group Work

Peer Assessment: Benefits of Group Work

Maryellen Weimer, PhD

Reason to read: One of the main benefits of asking students to work in groups is to expose them to feedback from one another. Read on to discover how peer feedback can improve group learning.

With the increased use of group work in college courses, exploration of the role of peer assessment has broadened, as has its use. In one survey, 57 percent of students reported that their faculty had incorporated peer evaluations into group assignments. We've done articles on this topic before, but mostly we've highlighted resources, specifically good instruments that direct peers to provide feedback in those areas known to influence group outcomes. Recent literature includes a variety of peer assessment systems (find three examples referenced at the end of this article), many of them online programs that expedite the collection, tabulation, and distribution of the results. Here's a list of the benefits of making peer assessment part of group learning experiences.

Peer assessment can prevent group process problems. Several studies show that it helps, and sometimes virtually solves, one of the most egregious group problems: free riding, as in students not doing their fair share of the work. One study found that the very possibility of having peer evaluations improved the performance of group members. Of course, that benefit is enhanced when peers receive feedback from each other as they are working together as opposed to when the project is finished.

Formative peer assessment also improves individual and group performance. Even if the group is not experiencing major problems, formative feedback from peers can help individual members fine-tune their contributions and help the group increase its overall effectiveness. Some of the processes faculty are using to achieve this benefit include individual and group responses to the feedback. Individual students comment on feedback from the group via an email to the teacher, and groups use the feedback to develop an improvement plan. They also make note of what the group is doing well. Online peer assessment systems make multiple exchanges of formative feedback possible, which is helpful when the groups are working on complex, course-long projects. The Brutus and Donia system resulted in measurable individual improvement during a second semester when the system was used. In other words, students took what they'd learned about their performance in the group and acted on it the following semester.

Peer assessment activities develop important professional skills. Students will be assessed by peers in most professional contexts. Group work experiences in college can "help them learn from others' observations of their behavior," according to Anson and Goodman (p. 27). That's a skill developed, not theoretically, but by actually getting some feedback and having to deal with it. And students need to learn how to deliver constructive feedback—what kind of comments motivate the desired behavior change and how those comments can be delivered without engendering excessive defensiveness. The rating systems described in the literature help students by identifying feedback areas and by proposing individual and group activities that should follow receipt of the feedback. Most of the online systems give teachers the opportunity to preview student feedback and comments before they are delivered to the group members.

Peers are in a position to provide valuable feedback. They are actually in a better position than the teacher, who, in the majority of cases, cannot be with all the groups all the time. Even if the teacher sees the group some of the time, peers see each other all the time. And peers see each other when individual members aren't trying to impress the teacher with their performance. Brutus and Donia go so far as to say "… peers possess a privileged viewpoint to evaluate performance." (p. 653)

Peer assessment adds credibility to the grading process. If peer assessments count, students start to take them seriously. And if faculty are using reliable and valid assessment systems, the data more accurately reflects what happened in the group than do the teacher assessments alone. Faculty are starting to recognize this benefit and incorporate peer assessments into the grading process. In the Brutus and Donia study, 74 percent of the faculty using their peer assessment system reported that they counted the peer assessments for between 5 and 50 percent of the grade calculation.

That's an impressive list of benefits, but they don't accrue automatically. Students aren't used to delivering or receiving feedback from peers.

That's why it's important to use a good feedback tool and make it part of a set of assessment activities and events.

RECOMMENDED REFERENCES:

Anson, R., and Goodman, J.A. (2014). A peer assessment system to improve student team experiences. *Journal of Education for Business, 89,* 27-34.

Brutus, S., and Donia, M. (2010). Improving the effectiveness of students in groups with a centralized peer evaluation system. *Academy of Management Learning and Education, 9* (4), 652-662.

Kemery, E.R., and Stickney, L.T. (2014). A multi-faceted approach to teamwork assessment in an undergraduate business program. *Journal of Management Education, 38* (3), 462-479.

Reprinted from *The Teaching Professor* newsletter, August/September 2014.

Structure, Video Conferencing Help Group Work Succeed

Rob Kelly

Reason to read: Even in the online space, group work can often be the best way for students to learn.

When Scotty Dunlap, assistant professor of safety, security, and emergency management at Eastern Kentucky University, surveyed his students about group work at the outset of an online graduate-level course on auditing, they unanimously gave it low ratings. Asked the same question at the end of the course, they all gave group work high marks. In an interview with *Online Classroom* newsletter, Dunlap explained how he structures group work and uses video conferencing to create effective teams and make group assignments an engaging and rewarding learning experience.

Contrary to what some students might think, instructors do not typically assign group work arbitrarily or maliciously. Group work can help prepare students for professional collaboration, and it facilitates peer learning. In some cases, it's simply the best way for students to learn.

One of the objectives of Dunlap's course is for students to create a tool to evaluate how well an organization is performing in any type of discipline related to safety, security, and emergency management. Ideally, this tool will also be useful to students in their careers.

Dunlap tried having students do this project individually. "That became overwhelming for a lot of students. In the eight weeks that this class takes place online, it's a pretty tough learning curve to get people through to the point where they not only know about auditing but can then actually apply it in this final project. Creating a group project reduced the [individual] workload significantly to where it was much more tolerable for each student while still achieving course learning outcomes," Dunlap says.

Unclear expectations within a group and lack of cohesiveness can detract from the online group learning experience. Dunlap tries to avoid these problems in several ways. In the second week of the course, facilitators—secondary instructors who each manage groups of 20 students—hold video conferences with each group (four or five students) to make sure that they're clear about assignment expectations, how the audit program is supposed to be set up, how the audit document is supposed to be created, and individual group members' responsibilities.

Dunlap likes to give students options on how they complete assignments. "I always try to give my students a lot of choice because I think they're going to learn better if they have control," he says. However, he has found that too much freedom can be an obstacle. In early iterations of this course, Dunlap explained the goals and end product and then let students select their groups and negotiate individual responsibilities. "We found that the process took way too much time. It may have been week three or four by the time a lot of that information was solidified, which left them with much less time to actually execute the project."

Now Dunlap assigns students to groups according to interest in a specific topic, minimizing time zone issues and providing a mix of experience levels. He has created documents that clearly explain the responsibilities for each group member. There is still some choice—each group member has different responsibilities—but providing this guidance has gotten groups off to a quicker start than when they are given total freedom to negotiate those roles.

In week five, facilitators convene a second video conference for each group to make sure that they are on track to complete the assignment. The video conference tool is also available to the groups for their independent use.

"It breaks down the technological divide a little bit because in all other online courses the only interaction students have with each other is through email or the discussion board. And so the students just become names on a computer screen. The video conferencing actually allows students to see, hear, and have an ongoing dialogue with people that ordinarily they would never have seen. It lowers a bit of the barrier that exists in a typical online class. It also allows for a much quicker avenue for students to ask questions, get directions, and set team member assignments, actions that otherwise would take place over a much longer period of time in the discussion board, their group space, or by email. So it's an efficiency issue as well," Dunlap says.

Technically, this course is totally asynchronous, so Dunlap does not require students to attend any video conferencing sessions. He does not penalize those who don't attend or reward those who do. Approximately 90 percent attend the facilitator-led video conferences and between one-quarter and one-half of groups use the video conferencing tool independently. This level of participation in the video conferences indicates this course feature's perceived value and, Dunlap says, has contributed to students' positive perception of group work at the end of the course.

"Their perception of group projects coming into this course was pretty hideous, which was expected because a lot of students just don't like doing group projects. But with the way we structured it by using video conferencing and allowing them to interact with each other, the students responded incredibly well by the end of it," Dunlap says.

RECOMMENDED REFERENCE:

Zambrano, R. "Online Course Activities to Increase Student Engagement." *Online Classroom (16)*12.

Reprinted from *Online Classroom* newsletter, March 2013.

Assessing Group Work in the College Classroom

Claire Howell Major, PhD

Reason to read: If you have ever struggled with grading group work, you will want to explore the following template for assessing group work.

Grading small group work can be a challenge. Most instructors use a combination of individual product and group product, often developing a percentage split based upon the assignment.

Many instructors also assess the processes of group work. They often do so by asking students to complete group and self-assessment. Following are sample forms for process assessment.

Sample Peer Evaluation Form for Small Group Work			
The team member	Needs Improvement = 1	Adequate = 2	Outstanding = 3
Prepares			
Listens			
Contributes			
Respects others			
Demonstrates the following skills:			
•Critical thinking			
•Problem solving			
•Communication			
•Decision making			
Subtotals			
Total			

Sample Self-Evaluation Form for Small Group Work	
Name _____ Group Number or ID _____ Project _____	
Rate yourself on your performance on the project using the following scale: 5 = Always 4 = Frequently 3 = Sometimes 2 = Rarely 1 = Never	
Performance Criteria	**Rating**
I was prepared to contribute to the group	
I stayed on task	
I listened to others	
I participated in discussion	
I encouraged others to participate	
Overall I felt my performance in the group should be rated:	

RECOMMENDED REFERENCE:

Howell Major, C. with E. F. Barkley and K. P. Cross. *Collaborative Learning Techniques: A Handbook for College Faculty.* 2014. San Francisco: Jossey Bass.

Adapted from the Magna Online Seminar, *Choosing and Using Group Activities in the College Classroom.*

How Do I Assign Students to Groups?

Ike Shibley, PhD

Reason to read: If you've ever struggled with getting all group members involved in an activity, then keep reading to find out how to successfully assign students to groups, grade group work, and more.

Group work is one of those areas that some business and engineering faculty think is essential because that's what those students will be doing in the workplace. I don't want to undermine that view, but I do want to say that there is more to group work than just getting ready for the working world. We learn better when we share our ideas with others. When we have to articulate those ideas, have others bounce those ideas back to us, and try to justify claims or statements that we're making, even in the hard sciences, there are many benefits that arise from working in a group.

If one student doesn't understand something, another student may be able to help the struggling student look at a concept in a slightly different way. Hearing different ways of thinking about information, in each of our courses, is critically important. Group work can completely change the dynamic of your class. Without spending a lot of time on the theory, I do want to encourage you to try group work.

The teacher in a group class is no longer the central person. Students will still look to you for guidance and grades, but they will start to build up positive interdependence. In other words, they start to trust each other and they start to rely on each other to help learn the information. When their gaze focuses on classmates instead of you, it can be a little discouraging because the students seem to learn without your direct assistance. But what you're doing is facilitating the effective functioning of groups. If you're teaching groups, one of the best ways to know whether you've created a great assignment is to see what happens when the students get to work. If the volume level rises, you know that students are starting to learn from each other and you've done a great job.

When we ask students about group work, they often say they enjoy learning from each other because they have to talk—because they have to share. This is active learning. Group work does not occur without activities, and activities are so named because students have to be actively engaged, wrestling with the content. It's essential that your group activities get everyone involved. It's not an easy skill to develop, but the more you work with groups, the better you'll be at finding ways to get everyone in the group working.

In some classes, working with groups is a great way to get immediate feedback. If you're doing problems in a math class, students can help each other. "Is this the right answer?" "No, that's not what I got." Have them check each other and look through to see what work is being done. The students can often help each other. You're there as a backup if the students say, "We can't figure out the difference." Now your role as a teacher is to help those students.

When I walk by classrooms where there is group work going on, there is a level of energy that is not present in a classroom where the teacher is at the board, lecturing with chalk and blackboard or a PowerPoint. The students seem much more passive in these lecture classes; they're not in control of their learning. That energy is missing. Group work can energize your students, and I think you'll find it can energize you as a teacher.

Why shift to group-based learning?
1. The workplace is changing. The business folks and the engineers who say, "Hey, students need to learn to work in groups," are right. Working in groups is an important skill for students to learn.
2. The student population is changing. Students are not coming to class anymore with the ability to sit for hours while you lecture at them. Students want to be actively engaged. As much as we complain about the video generation, the fact is that the more that you actively engage students, getting them to wrestle with concepts in your course, the better their learning is going to be. They're rehearsing while they're doing it. They need to challenge themselves to get a better sense of where their limitations are and where they have to work outside of class.
3. The teaching paradigm is changing. The shift from being teacher-centered to learner-centered is critically important in all this. We

know from the pedagogical research that teachers who find ways of engaging students are the ones who have students who perform better on exams, writing assignments, and group presentations. These are students who are learning more. In a learner-centered classroom, the student learns more.

Types of groups

There are "completely cooperative" groups where students get graded together—they have to do everything together, and they turn in one assignment. A "cooperative" assignment is usually on in which students work together but they turn in graded material individually. An example is a laboratory setting where students have to set up and do the lab together but write individual reports.

"Helping permitted" refers to when students take individual exams but work on them in a group during class; if one of them doesn't understand something, they are allowed to help each other. "Peer mentoring," then, is where more experienced students in a class work with other students in a mentoring relationship. In these cases, the students are really working with each other within a group.

Grouping styles

Do you want to facilitate heterogeneous or homogeneous grouping? Do you want students with similar majors, similar interests, or similar grade points to be grouped together? Do you want to do the grouping? Do you want to allow students to group themselves? And if you do group, do you want your groups to be random, or do you want to assign them? Obviously, if it's random, it's likely going to be heterogeneous grouping, but you run the risk of getting a homogeneous group as well. If you don't care about heterogeneity verses homogeneity, maybe you want to group randomly. If you assign groups, you need to think about how you want to assign them.

Do you want students to do work outside of class, or do you want it all done in class? Or do you not want to do any in class and only outside of class? The clearer you are about your expectations for groups, the better the students will be able to understand.

Do you plan formal or informal groups? A formal group is a stable group, one that is either assigned or self-selected. These students meet with that group throughout the semester. An informal group is better when you have lots of different students in a given class. These groups are chosen randomly, but the groups only work together for one class period or so before disbanding. Informal groups provide a lot of benefits, and you can accomplish different goals with informal groups than you can with formal groups.

Grading

Do you want to assign one grade? Do you want completely cooperative learning, or do you want something more collaborative where you assign individual grades but the students still work together? You have to answer questions like these before getting into group work.

Low-stakes grading can work well with informal groups. You can work with a pass/fail system, or you can assign a low number of points to the assignments informal groups tackle. You just want to make sure the students have some incentive to actually get together and do the work. In a formal group, though, I can't emphasize enough the need for rubrics. You also need to think about giving students a chance to assess one another. Get some ideas together for how to let students assess each other. Students want to know that if they're in a group, fair grading criteria will apply, and you want to relieve some of the anxiety students have with groups.

I hope I've convinced you to at least try assigning group work. Please read some of the recommended references that I've provided below, and use some of these ideas. Try groups. Make sure you have clear goals so that you know what you want the groups to do. And make your grading policies as clear as possible. You cannot get away with just telling students, "Oh, we'll figure out how you're going to be graded." You need to have clear rubrics—your groups will work much better.

RECOMMENDED REFERENCES:

Bruffee, K. A. (1993). *Collaborative learning: Higher education, interdependence, and the authority of knowledge.* Baltimore, MD: Johns Hopkins Press.

Johnson, D. W., Johnson, R. T., & Holubec, E. J. (1994). *The new circles of learning: Cooperation in the classroom and school.* Alexandria, VA: Association for Supervision of Curriculum and Development.

Millis, B. J. and Cottell, P. G. (1998). Cooperative learning for higher education faculty. Phoenix, AZ: Oryx Press.

Stodolsky, S. S. (1984). In the social context of interaction: Group organization and group processes. Peterson, P. L., Wilkinson, L. C., and

Hallinan, M. (Eds.), *The Social Context of Instruction* (pp. 107–124). San Diego, CA: Academic Press.

Adapted from the Magna 20-Minute Mentor presentation, *How Do I Assign Students to Groups?*

Group Work: Collaborative, Cooperative, or Problem-Based?

Maryellen Weimer, PhD

Reason to read: If you've ever been the slightest bit perplexed by the differences between collaborative, cooperative, and problem-based learning, have no fear: The author covers each type and the drawbacks and benefits of each.

Recent interest in using group work to promote learning and develop important interpersonal skills began in the late '80s, and since then, various types of group work have been promoted, researched, and implemented. Among the most widely used and best known "brands" are collaborative learning, cooperative learning, and problem-based learning. An outstanding article in a recent issue of the *Journal on Excellence in College Teaching* devoted to exploring group work looks in detail at these three approaches.

Despite widespread familiarity with the terms, collaborative, cooperative, and problem-based learning have been consistently muddled, mixed up, and used imprecisely to describe what students are doing in small groups. This inaccurate use of the terms has confounded practitioners' understanding of these forms of group work and the relationship between them.

Added to this definitional confusion is the fact that each of these forms of group work has had loyal advocates who've trumpeted one of the three over the other two. As a result, those who use cooperative learning or problem-based learning know little about collaborative learning. And those devoted to the collaborative approach don't use the other two. Few with an affinity for one of these three have much familiarity with the other two, and this exclusivity is one of the motivations for this article. Authors Neil

Davidson and Claire Major wonder whether it's time for those using these three types of group work to start learning from each other. Their aim is not to be prescriptive, but descriptive. "What makes this article unique is its invitation to practitioners to cross traditional boundaries, to consider similarities and differences of these approaches, and to begin productive conversations that can advance the field of small-group learning." (p. 11)

These three approaches to group work do share certain features. Each starts with a common task or learning activity that can be completed by students working together in a group. Students talk (face-to-face or online) to each other about the task or activity they've been assigned to complete in each approach. They work together cooperatively. In each of these group structures, students are individually accountable for what they learn and what they contribute to the group's learning goal.

But each of these forms of group work has distinct features not shared by the others, and these differences are explored in lengthy detail in this article. Here's a nutshell summary of some of features that make each unique. "Cooperative learning is more structured and employs more active teacher facilitation than collaborative learning." (p. 32) Problem-based learning is organized similarly to cooperative learning, with the key difference being its exclusive focus on problems. Collaborative learning relies on more open-ended interaction, with the goal being the discovery, understanding, or production of knowledge. (p. 21) In cooperative learning, roles may be assigned. They usually aren't in collaborative learning, and group interaction skills are not generally taught as part of collaborative learning activities. In cooperative learning, teachers usually form the groups, while in collaborative learning students form the groups themselves. Collaborative learning groups are mostly self-managed. Problem-based learning groups tend to be larger than the other two.

The use of these three forms of group work has followed disciplinary lines. Collaborative learning has been mostly used in the humanities and some in the social sciences but rarely in the sciences or professional programs. Cooperative learning has been mostly used in the sciences, math, engineering, the social sciences, and professional programs. PBL has been used across disciplines but was developed for use in medical education, and it is still most commonly associated with the health professions. The match between group structure and discipline has not received much attention in the literature. One could conjecture that the association derives from how knowledge in these disciplines is organized, how it is discovered, and how it advances.

The association between group work type and discipline has had other implications as well. Collaborative learning has not been studied much empirically, whereas cooperative learning and PBL have received extensive empirical attention and with generally impressive results. The article highlights "strong evidence ... that students working in small groups outperform their counterparts in a number of key areas. These include knowledge development, thinking skills, social skills and course satisfaction." (p. 7)

In addition to the slim analysis of collaborative learning, the authors point out that research has not explored the optimal sequencing of group experiences. "We argue that exposing students to problem-solving learning in sequence from more structured to less structured will provide scaffolding to prepare them to succeed." (p. 45) They then offer a variety of ways this sequencing could be investigated.

Possibly the most compelling part of this article is how its analysis of the evidence clarifies the long-debated relations between these three forms of group work. "The cooperative learning approaches all employ certain elements which are not used by the collaborative teachers and which are not accepted by them. Hence, cooperative learning is not a form of collaborative learning (and vice versa). Likewise, PBL is not a form of either. Cooperative learning, collaborative learning, and PBL are all forms of small-group learning and have some major points in common. However, none of the approaches is a special case of any of the others." (p. 32) Table 2 on pages 33 and 34 lays out the differences and similarities that make each a related but separate form of group work.

The article reviews the literature and research of those who have advocated and studied each of these forms of group work. Ironically, many faculty who use group work are not familiar with either the advocates or the research. These are faculty who have learned to use group work the same way they learned to teach: by trial and error. They are using group work in ways that creatively integrate and combine these three (and other) approaches to group work, providing real-world examples of just how much advocates of a particular form of group work could be learning from each other.

RECOMMENDED REFERENCE:

Davidson, N., and Major, C. H. (2014). Boundary crossings: Cooperative learning, collaborative learning and problem-based learning. *Journal on Excellence in College Teaching, 25* (3 and 4), 7-55.

Reprinted from *The Teaching Professor* newsletter, February 2015.

What Components Make Group Work Successful?

Maryellen Weimer, PhD

Reason to read: Explore the research behind what makes group work work.

There's lots of research documenting the positive effects of group experiences on learning outcomes. We've highlighted many of these studies in previous issues of the newsletter. Less is known about the specific aspects of group experiences that contribute to their overall positive impact. Thomas Tomcho and Rob Foels decided to explore this question by looking at the research on group learning in the field of psychology, as reported in the journal *Teaching of Psychology.*

In order to conduct a meta-analytic review of that research, they needed to identify those specific aspects of group work that might affect how much and how well students learned in groups. They looked at research on group processes and at studies of collaborative learning both inside and outside psychology. From the group processes research and literature, they identified three components believed to influence learning outcomes in groups: the size of the group, how long the group interacted, and the complexity of the task completed by the group. From the collaborative learning research and literature, five aspects of group experiences with potential positive effects emerged: pre-activity preparation (group members coming to the activity after having done something to prepare for it, such as completing a worksheet or answering a set of discussion questions); participant interdependence; peer assessment; group accountability (as illustrated by having to do something jointly, such as a group presentation); and individual accountability (as shown by something such as a written assignment accompanying the group experience).

Given the general consensus in the literature that these specific features of group work positively affect learning outcomes, the next question is how those effects on learning were measured. To be considered in this review, the impact on learning had to have been assessed in one of the four following ways: via a pre- and post-test knowledge measure with a control and experimental group; a self-reported change in attitude or belief; a change in skill or behavior (perhaps the quality of a writing sample); or the relation of the activity to exam, assignment, or course grades.

The findings of this meta-analysis are based on a comparison of the results in 37 studies published between 1974 and 2011 in *Teaching of Psychology*. To be included in the analysis, studies had to meet the five criteria of methodological rigor explained in the article.

And the findings contained some surprises—some results did not confirm these researchers' hypotheses. "Despite deriving predictions from the group processes and collaborative learning literatures regarding several potential moderators, we found that only group duration, participant interdependence, peer assessment, and group accountability predicted learning outcomes (with the latter two in a negative direction)" (p. 2012, 165). In other words, the size of the group didn't affect learning outcomes, nor did the complexity of the task completed by the group. Learning outcomes were also not influenced by whether students prepared beforehand for the group activity or by individual accountability. If a peer assessment procedure was used and groups had to make presentations, that had a negative effect on learning in those groups. As for group duration, the strongest positive effect was found for groups that met for a comparatively brief period of time, as in one to three class sessions.

Why wouldn't having to do something such as making a presentation increase the learning potential of those within that group? The results don't answer the question, but the researchers wonder if that result might be explained by the fact that when a presentation must be done, groups often simply divide the presentation into parts and assign each member a different part. In that case, students learn their part but not the parts being presented by others. That problem can be addressed by designing group projects that cannot be partitioned into independent parts—something the researchers recommend.

This article reports the analysis of research on group work in one field, and the authors identify some empirical issues that may implicate these findings. Pedagogical scholarship does not systematically follow a line of research, with findings related and building on each other, and that makes integrating a collection of studies challenging. So the value of this work is not its generalizability across disciplines but in the questions it raises about why group work promotes learning and what design features do and don't influence the learning outcomes. When most faculty design group activities, decisions about group formation and duration, the nature of the task, final products, and assessment methods are based on assumptions—what we think might help the groups be successful and enrich the learning experience. If nothing else, this research should encourage us to explore the premises on which those assumptions rest and consider how we might assess the impact of these features of group work on the learning experiences of our students.

RECOMMENDED REFERENCE:

Tomcho, T. J., and Foels, R. 2012. "Meta-Analysis of Group Learning Activities: Empirically Based Teaching Recommendations." *Teaching of Psychology, 39* (3): 159–169.

Reprinted from *The Teaching Professor* newsletter, November 2012.

An Interesting Group Work Model

Maryellen Weimer, PhD

Reason to read: In the POGIL model, the instructor functions as a facilitator who's available to assist the groups, although students are expected to figure out the answers to most questions on their own.

It has a long, not-easy-to-remember name: Process Oriented Guided Inquiry Learning. It usually goes by its acronym: POGIL. It's a model designed to replace lectures (though not necessarily all of them). Students discuss course material in teams, and they use carefully designed material that involves sequenced sets of questions—that's the guided-inquiry part of the model. The process part relates to what is generally a three-phase learning cycle that involves exploration, invention, and application. It is derived from Piaget's work on mental functioning.

In the exploration phase, students usually start with a model and the questions help them see patterns within the model. "Often, the questions lead students to test hypotheses or explain the patterns and relationships found in the model." (p. 263) The invention phase involves introduction of a concept or relationship. In the application phase, students are challenged to extend and apply the concept to new situations. "The sequence of questions in POGIL materials are carefully devised to help students progress properly through the phases, to guide them toward appropriate conclusions, and to develop desired process skills, such as problem solving, deductive reasoning, communication and self-assessment." (p. 236)

The POGIL model was developed for use in the sciences and has been used successfully in a variety of chemistry courses; in biology, anatomy and physiology, physics, math, computer science, and environmental science; and now in other fields such as education and marketing. The website (http://pogil.org) shows sample materials. For those interested in the model, the website contains much useful information, including a detailed instructor's guide that can be downloaded for free.

In this model, the instructor functions as a facilitator who's available to assist the groups. However, instructors do not answer questions that students should be able to figure out for themselves. Rather than answering student questions, instructors opt to ask the group questions that lead them to the answer. Students are assigned roles in this model. There is some variation in the roles, but there might be a manager who keeps the group on task, a scribe who is the group's official record keeper, a spokesperson who may be called upon to share the group's solution, and a librarian who may be the only person in the group permitted to have the textbook open.

The POGIL model has been studied empirically in a number of courses. Here's a sample of the findings. In organic chemistry, less than 8 percent of more than 1,000 students were negative about the method. The same cohort had 30 percent registering negative attitudes about traditional lectures. In an anatomy and physiology course, grades improved at significant levels. In a medicinal chemistry course taken by pharmacy students, exam scores for students in the POGIL section were higher, as was the final grade distribution (see reference at the end of this article).

This not a method that can be undertaken without significant planning and preparation. The anatomy and physiology professor writes, "Although POGIL requires a great deal of effort and a careful introduction to students who might be skeptical of a novel and unfamiliar classroom experience, its benefits cannot be easily disputed."

Reference: Eberlein, T., Kampmeier, J., et. al (2008). Pedagogies of engagement in science: A comparison on PBL, POGIL, and PLTL. *Biochemistry and Molecular Biology Education, 36* (4), 262-273.

RECOMMENDED REFERENCES:

Brown, P. J. P. (2010). Process-oriented guided-inquiry learning in an introductory anatomy and physiology course with a diverse student population. *Advances in Physiology Education, 34,* 150-155.

Brown, S. D. (2010). A process-oriented guided inquiry approach to teaching medicinal chemistry. *American Journal of Pharmaceutical Education, 74* (4), article 121.

Reprinted from *The Teaching Professor* newsletter, April 2011.

Facilitating Small Group Activities with Google Drive

Matthew P. Winslow, PhD

Reason to read: Online group work comes with its own set of challenges. Now grading doesn't have to be one of them.

Faculty are always on the lookout for a good system for facilitating group work. You want a system that separates student contributions and allows the instructor to view the progression of student work. Google Drive, a cloud-based, shared document editing website, is ideal for this purpose. Its power lies in the ability of collaborators to edit the exact same document in real time. There are no more problems with multiple versions floating around in email attachments. You can even watch edits being made by different collaborators at once with different-colored cursors moving across the screen making edits.

Another nice feature of Drive is that work is saved without hitting any save button. As soon as you enter a keystroke on the computer, the work is saved. Because it is cloud-based, work does not need to be submitted to another location for the instructor to see it. The instructor is just given access to work as a shared collaborator, and can add his or her feedback directly to that work.

Drive comes with the myriad of features you are offered when creating a Google account, including email, word processing, spreadsheet, presentation, blogging, website hosting, a YouTube page, audio- and videoconferences through Google+ Hangouts, and a variety of other services, all for free. You need not use them all and can activate only those you want. Google also has the very powerful Google Classroom available free for any institution. It requires an institutional account to activate, but it is well worth asking your institution to pursue.

You can create files on Drive by either uploading files made on other systems, such as Word, Excel, or PowerPoint, or creating them from scratch on the Drive site. The person who creates or uploads the file is designated as its "owner" and can then share access to it with other users via their Gmail accounts. The owner can also designate the access privileges of each user, with some given the ability to only view the work, others given the ability to edit it, and others given the ability to delete it as a co-owner.

Drive's word processing, spreadsheet, and presentation features are similar to those on PC or Mac systems, so there is almost no learning curve for most users. What is new to most students is simultaneous editing. Students may at first feel nervous about directly editing someone else's work, and so instead they make suggestions using the comments feature. This is fine, but the ideal group collaboration is when there is enough trust and comfort for people to directly add to the shared document.

Another helpful feature of Google Drive is revision history. This allows instructors to look back at the history of the file and see individuals' contributions. Different users' contributions show up in different colors.

Step-by-step guide to using Google Drive for a group project:
1. Instruct students to create a Google account and send you a Gmail from that account in order to get their address.
2. Save each incoming student's email as a contact in order to make it easier to share files with them in Drive.
3. Create a contact group within your Google account for each group of students. This will make it easier to contact all group members at once by email. Take a look at this tutorial on how to create Google groups: bit.ly/1icfoqk.
4. If you want to give each group a template to scaffold their work, or perhaps questions to answer, then upload that to Drive.
5. Save a copy of that template for each group with a different name (group 1, group 2, etc.).
6. Give each group access to its own version by adding group members as editors through the sharing feature.
7. Check each group's progress periodically, using the revision history to assess individual contributions, and make comments when needed.
8. Once the assignment is due, add feedback on the Drive version itself, or download it to your learning management system.

Google Drive is a simple, powerful system for facilitating online group work. Use it for group assignments in your courses.

RECOMMENDED REFERENCE:

Orlando, J. "Online Learning 2.0: Google Drive Is Your New Best Friend." *Online Classroom (14)12.*

Reprinted from *Online Classroom* newsletter, November 2015.

Choosing an Approach for Small Group Work

Claire Howell Major, PhD

Reason to read: Here it is: everything you need to consider when considering using group work in your class.

Try the term "group work" in a Google search, and you'll find yourself bombarded with dozens of hits clustered around definitions of group work, benefits of group work, and educational theories underpinning group work. If you dig a little deeper into the links you return, however, you'll find that not all of the pages displayed under the moniker of "group work" describe the same thing. Instead, dozens of varieties of group learning appear. They all share the common feature of having students work together, but they have different philosophies, features, and approaches to the group task.

Does it matter what we call it? Maryellen Weimer asked this important question in her *Teaching Professor* article (2014) of the same title, with the implicit idea that one approach might be better suited for a given task than another. She believes that the answer to the question is yes. And she's right. As the adage goes, it is important to choose the right tool for the job at hand. A hammer is not the best tool for drilling a hole, and a drill is not the best tool for driving a nail. Both are good tools, when used for the appropriate job. So it is with group work. If you don't choose the best possible approach, then you will be less likely to accomplish the goals and objectives of the assignment.

While there are several different forms of group work, there are a few that are more often used than others and that have a body of research that supports their effectiveness. Three of these are cooperative learning, collaborative learning, and reciprocal peer teaching.

Cooperative learning

In this form of group learning, students work together in a small group so that everyone participates on a collective task that has been clearly assigned (Cohen 1994, 3). A classic example of this approach is Think-Pair-Share (Barkley, Major, and Cross 2014), in which the teacher assigns a question, and then students think for a minute independently, form a pair to discuss their answers, and share their answers with a larger group. The goal is that all students achieve similar outcomes. Each student considers the same teacher-assigned question, and they all work on performing the same tasks: thinking, pairing, and sharing.

Collaborative learning

In this form of group learning, students and faculty work together to make create knowledge. The process should enrich and enlarge them (Matthews1996, 101). An example of this form of group work is a collaborative paper (Barkley, Major, and Cross 2014). In a collaborative group, students work together to create a product that is greater than any individual might achieve alone. They do not all necessarily do the same task, however, but rather, may divide work among themselves according to interests and skills. The goal is not for the same learning to occur, but rather that meaningful learning occurs.

Reciprocal peer teaching

In this form of group learning, one student teaches others, who then reciprocate in kind (Major, Harris, and Zakrajsek 2015). It is possible to argue that this approach is a variation of either cooperative learning or collaborative learning, depending on the task. An example that leans more toward cooperative learning is the Jigsaw, in which base groups study together to become experts (Barkley, Major, and Cross 2014). The base groups then split, and new groups are formed with a member of each base group serving as an expert in particular area. An example that leans more toward collaborative learning is microteaching, in which individual students take turns teaching the full class (Major, Harris, and Zakrajsek 2015).

These three approaches are all tried and true group-learning varieties. They all have been shown to benefit students on a number of outcomes, from the acquisition of content knowledge to the development of higher order thinking skills (Davidson and Major 2014). How is it possible, then, to choose the right pedagogical tool for the learning task?

Pedagogical considerations

In choosing any approach to group learning, it is essential to start with the learning goal. What should students be able to do after the completion of the activity? If the goal is for them all to gain the same information, cooperative learning may be the best approach. If the goal is for them to create new knowledge, then collaborative learning may be the best approach. If it is to share knowledge, reciprocal peer teaching may be a good approach.

Learner considerations

When making any pedagogical consideration, it is essential to consider the students. Their level of expertise is important, for example, and if they are new to a subject and need foundational knowledge, then cooperative learning may be the best approach. If they are advanced students, then collaborative learning or reciprocal peer teaching may be more engaging for them.

Contextual considerations

While contextual considerations are not always the most glamorous, they certainly play a part in our ability to carry out group work. For example, if the class is a large one, a short collaborative activity such as a Think-Pair-Share may simply be more manageable than a long-term collaborative activity; likewise, reciprocal microteaching may be a great approach in an online class but would not be as feasible in a large lecture. A collaborative paper might be a great way to introduce graduate seminar students who work as research assistants at a flagship university to the process of co-authoring, but the same approach might not work as well for first-year students at a commuter college.

As teachers, we need to know what the instructional options are and to take into account the goals, the learners, and the learning context when making pedagogical decisions. Ultimately, it is our responsibility to choose well when deciding to use group work in the college classroom.

RECOMMENDED REFERENCE:

Jacoby, B. *Seven Strategies to Enhance Learning through Group Work*. Magna Online Seminar. www.magnapubs.com/online-seminars/seven-strategies-to-enhance-learning-through-group-work-3083-1.html

Reprinted from *Faculty Focus*, September 21, 2015.

APPENDIX

•

Tools and Templates

Strategies That Increase the Number of Students Who Participate in Class

Maryellen Weimer, PhD

- Increase your wait time.
- Talk about how you think discussion is better when many students participate.
- Get students to discuss what makes participation a valuable learning experience for them.
- Don't let some students participate too often.
- Listen carefully when students speak and thank them for their contributions.
- Focus on students when they are speaking.
- Look directly and encouragingly at students who don't speak.
- Use something the student said in your follow-up commentary.
- Ask a thought-provoking question and give students 30 seconds to jot down some ideas.
- Put the question (or part of it) on the board or in a PowerPoint presentation.
- Ask an important question and then let students briefly talk about it with those nearby.
- If a student offers a great explanation or has an interesting idea, label it with the student's name and refer to it subsequently. Do your best to find something positive to say about a first-time contribution.
- Take care when responding to wrong or not-very-good answers.
- Don't always have the right answer to every question.
- Talk informally with students before class begins, after it's over, when you see students on campus or via email.
- Define participation broadly.
- Expect great answers.

Learning More about Participation

A lot of good research has been done on participation in college class-rooms. Here are some key findings that provide excellent background and reasons why working to get more students participating is so important.

- In an observational study of 20 social science and humanities class-rooms, teachers devoted only 5.85% of total class time to student participation. That's approximately one minute per 40 minutes of class time.
- Half the students surveyed in this study said they participated infrequently or never in classes.

Reference: Nunn, C. E. "Discussion in the College Classroom: Triangulating Observational and Survey Results." *Journal of Higher Education*, 1996, 67 (3), 243–266.

- In another observational study, only 44% of the students participated, and 28% of those who did participate accounted for 89% of all the comments made by students.

Reference: Howard, J. R., Short, L. B., and Clark, S. M. "Students' Participation in the Mixed Age Classroom." *Teaching Sociology*, 1996, 24 (1), 8–24.

- Why students don't participate: One study found that the main reason is a lack of confidence. Students feared looking unintelligent in front of the professor and in front of their peers.

Reference: Fassinger, P. A. "Understanding Classroom Interaction: Students' and Professors' Contributions to Students' Silence." *Journal of Higher Education*, 1995, 66 (1), 82–96.

- "The more students perceive the professor as an authority of knowledge, the less likely it is they will participate in class." (p. 586)
- Traditional-age students (defined as those between 18 and 24) are 2.5 times more likely to report that they never or seldom participate in class than non-traditional-age students. And non-traditional-age students are three times more likely to report that they always participate.
- Noted as the most important finding: Faculty interaction outside the class positively influences participation in class.

Reference: Weaver, R. R. and Qi, Jiang. "Classroom Organization and Participation." *Journal of Higher Education*, 2005, 76 (5), 570–600.

- Less participation occurred in introductory courses than in upper-division courses: 5.7 students made two or more comments and contributed 75% of all student comments in the introductory courses observed, and 8.5 students made two or more comments for 90% of all student comments in the upper-division courses.

Reference: Fritschner, L. M. "Inside the Undergraduate College Classroom: Faculty and Students Differ on the Meaning of Student Participation." *Journal of Higher Education*, 2000, 71 (3), 342–362.

- Observers noted 31 interactions per session, 29 (92%) of which were made by 5 students.
- 29.3% of students were defined as "talkers" — they made two or more contributions per class session.
- More than half the students did not participate in any of the 10 sessions of each class observed.

Reference: Howard, J. R. and Henney, A. C. "Student Participation and Instructor Gender in Mixed Age Classrooms." *Journal of Higher Education*, 1998, 69 (4), 384–405.

- Only a bit more than 50% of the nontalkers (defined as students who did not speak or contributed fewer than two comments per class session) thought that students had a responsibility to participate in discussion.
- A student view repeatedly expressed during interviews: "Students, as consumers, have purchased the right to choose a passive role if they wish. To make them uncomfortable by requiring they participate in discussion was deemed an unreasonable expectation by many of the students interviewed." (p. 516)
- Only 43% of students (about 30% of the nontalkers) thought it was fair for an instructor to make verbal participation a part of the grade.

Reference: Howard, J. R. and Baird, R. "The Consolidation of Responsibility and Students' Definitions of Situation in the Mixed Age College Classroom." *Journal of Higher Education*, 2000, 71 (6), 700–721.

- Students overestimate the level at which they participate. More than 56% identified themselves "talkers," defined in this study as students making more than two contributions per class session. Just about 26% of these students were "talkers," based on observations of them in the classroom.

Reference: Howard, J. R., James, G. H., and Taylor, D. R. "The Consolidation of Responsibility in the Mixed Age Classroom." *Teaching Sociology*, 2002, 30, 214–234

Adapted from the Magna 20-Minute Mentor program, *How Do I Get More Students to Participate in Class?*

Sample Discussion Rubric

John Orlando, PhD

20 Points Maximum

	A 18–20 points total	B 16–17 points total	C 14–15 points total	D/F 0 points	Points
Subject Knowledge and Integration of Research Materials	Excellent grasp and integration of course material; information from readings or outside sources integrated and cited appropriately in posts.	Sound grasp of material from assigned readings in initial statement. Some use of outside sources, appropriately cited.	Familiarity with most material and principles in the discussion. Lacking substantive use of outside sources. Incorrect or absent citations.	Poor grasp of material and principles in the discussion. Little or no use of outside sources.	
Critical Analysis of Topic	High level of analysis; adds new ideas to discussion or asks highly relevant questions. Provides useful and substantive criticism to fellow group members.	Sound analysis of discussion issue and peripheral issues. Adds new ideas to discussion. Provides helpful feedback to group members.	Missed some of the main issues. Analysis simplistic or sketchy. Little substantive feedback provided to group members.	Little or no real analysis; undue reliance on unsubstantiated opinion and anecdotes. No substantive feedback to group members.	

Effective Writing	Able to clearly organize and articulate thoughts, ideas and opinions; few or no errors.	Writing is clear and easy to follow; some errors in spelling and grammar.	Overall writing in terms of structure, grammar, and spelling is barely acceptable.	Poor writing overall with awkward or confusing word usage. Many errors in grammar and spelling.	
Timely and Complete Participation	Timing, length, and number of posts exceed minimum standards; quality of posts is high and contributes greatly to the overall substance of the discussion.	Timing, length, and number of posts meet standards. Quality of posts adds to substance of the discussion.	Posts are late, too short, or infrequent. Regardless of quality, they may add little to the discussion because of late submission.	Posts are infrequent and appear too late in the week to enable other students to respond.	
Total Points Possible	**4–3.6 each**	**3.4–3.2 each**	**3–2.8 each**	**0 each**	

Total Points _____

Reprinted from the white paper, *How to Effectively Assess Online Learning*, 2011.

Learner-Centered Teaching: Where Should I Start?

Maryellen Weimer, PhD

Strategy 1: Creating the climate for learning

- Use the same activity but with a different topic. For example, before the first discussion in a class, you might have students talk about the best and worst class discussions they've observed. Again have them talk about what the teacher did and what the students did.
- The activity can be used as an icebreaker for group work. Say you've put students together in work groups. Have them start to get to know each other by talking about the best and worst group experiences they've had and what they need to do individually and collectively to have this group function well.
- At the end of the best/worse course discussion, ask a student to take a picture of the board (constructive use of cell phone in class) and send it to you. Then you can send a copy to each student. Obviously, you can write down what students said and distribute a paper or electronic copy.
- Use the description of the best class as an early course feedback mechanism. During the second or third week of the course, have students rate the items they listed. Say that they said, "The teacher respects students"; ask them to rate on a five-point scale how well that's happening in class so far. You might rate them on some of the student characteristics.

Strategy 2: Let the students summarize

- Give students a few minutes to review their notes, and then on the board or in a PowerPoint presentation share what you consider the three most important points. Have students check to see how many of these points they had in their notes. This is a good way to start involving students in summarizing activities. Don't use this approach every day, or students will just wait for your list, and chances are that's all that will end up in their notes.
- Use the summary points to start the next period. Ask a verbally confident student to read and briefly explain the three summary points

to another student who wasn't in class Monday. (I use the absent student's name.)
- Give students two or three sample questions based on the day's material and ask them to read (verbatim) what they have in their notes relevant to the question. This is a great strategy for showing students that often they don't write down enough in their notes.

Strategy 3: Lessons learned from the first exam
- Ask students to identify a study strategy they used that they think worked well and would recommend to other students. Do the opposite: Ask students to identify something they did or didn't do that didn't work well and that they don't plan to use again and wouldn't recommend to a fellow student.
- If returning the actual exam, have students look at how many times they changed answers and how often the strategy helped or hurt them.
- If students want another multiple-choice option to count, have them make the case by reading what they have in their notes or what appears in the text that supports that option. You can listen respectfully to their opinions, but you want to hear evidence.

RECOMMENDED REFERENCES:

DiClementi, J. D. and Handelsman, M. M. "Empowering Students: Class-Generated Rules." *Teaching of Psychology*, 2005, 32 (1), 18-21. Litz, R. A. "Red Light, Green Light and Other Ideas for Class Participation-Intensive Courses: Methods and Implications for Business Ethics Education." Teaching Business Ethics, 2003, 7 (4), 365–378.

Ludy, B. T. "Setting Course Goals: Privileges and Responsibilities in a World of Ideas." *Teaching of Psychology*, 2005, 32 (3), 146–149

Adapted from the Magna 20-Minute Mentor program, *How Do I Get More Students to Participate in Class?*

Activities to Create a Climate for Learning

Maryellen Weimer, PhD

Consider letting students set one or some classroom policies

If this seems to radical and you aren't sure what processes you might use, I'd recommend taking a look at the following article. The authors describe how they identified the areas where they thought policies were needed, put students in groups and let the groups propose a policy. For the first couple of times, they had students propose the policies but reserved the right not to accept what students proposed. They were afraid students might propose something not appropriate, but to their surprise students rose to challenge and recommended very legitimate policies. I have had the same experience. I let students set the participation policy in my courses. They come up with policies pretty much like the ones I used for years. But I must say, when students own a policy, it changes the climate in the classroom.

References: DiClementi, J. D. and Handelsman, M. M. "Empowering Students: Class-Generated Rules." *Teaching of Psychology,* 2005, *32* (1), 18–21.
Weimer, M. *Learner-Centered Teaching: Five Key Changes to Practice.* San Francisco: Jossey-Bass, 2002. See pp. 34–37.

Getting students acquainted with each other early on in the course

Climates for learning are personal spaces. Students need to know each other and teachers need know the students. This process should be started early in the course. In the June-July, 2008 issue of the *Teaching Professor,* education professor Karen Eifler describes the unique approach she uses. She calls it "academic speed dating." Students sit in two rows facing each other (more rows of two if the class is large) holding a copy of the syllabus. The partners facing each other must answer two questions, read to them by the professor, one about the syllabus and the other about themselves. Students have 2-3 minutes to answer both questions. Then students in one of the rows move down one seat and the process is repeated. This is one of those great strategies that kills two birds with one stone—it gets students looking for important information in the syllabus and sharing information about themselves with each other. Eifler finishes with a debrief discussion to make sure everybody has gotten the correct syllabus information.

A Graffiti needs assessment

Barbara Goza developed this first day of class activity. She posts pieces of newsprint on the walls around the classroom. Each newsprint contains the beginning of a sentence. Those sentences may inquire about all sorts of things of interest to the instructor and fellow classmates. "In a nutshell, here is what I know about (fill in the name/content of your course." "Here's what's worrying me most about this class. . ." "I learn best in classes where the teacher. . ." Here's what my classmates can do that will help me learn in this class. . ." The sky is really the limit with respect to the prompts. Goza gives her students 15 minutes during which they walk around the room and fill in answers to the prompts. You could certainly encourage students to chat with each other while they are doing this. As Goza goes through the usual first day details, she refers to responses the students have written, raising questions about them, offering clarifying material, addressing concerns, etc.

Reference: Goza, B. K. "Graffiti Needs Assessment: Involving Students in the First Class Session." *Journal of Management Education,* 1993, *17* (1), 99–106.

Letting students work on developing grading rubrics

Whether you call them rubrics or grading criteria, they are the guidelines you use to determine the relative merit of a piece of student work. When students work with you on developing them, they get a very clear answer to their frequent query, "What do you want in this assignment?" You can have them work with you developing a rubric as a whole class or they can work on generating the criteria a small groups. If students haven't had much experience doing this, it helps if they have some models. If you use some of the criteria students suggest, they gives them a role in the grading process and we're back to another activity that helps to create a climate for learning in the classroom. If you aren't familiar with rubrics or would like a quick and helpful review, I'd recommend this article.

Reference: Andrade, H. G. "Teaching with Rubrics: The Good, the Bad, and the Ugly." *College Teaching,* 2005, *53* (1), 27–30.

Adapted from the Magna 20-Minute Mentor Program, *How Do I Get More Students to Participate in Class?*

How Do I Prepare to Team-teach a Course?

Ike Shibley, PhD

CHECKLISTS

How to Decide Whether to Team-Teach
- Examine how collaboration could help the students
- Determine if a collaborator is interested
- Consider compatibility with your team teacher
- List potential topics for course
- Talk about pedagogical philosophy

How to prepare
- Start by visiting each other's classes and pay careful attention to the pedagogy (see the 'Classroom Observation by Colleague' on the following pages)
- Collaboratively establish learning outcomes: broad course-specific goals that drive the creation of learning goals
- Collaboratively establish learning goals: specific goals for each topic with active verbs
- Plan an outline of possible topics
- Discuss grading components including the weight of each component, how to grade, views on attendance
- Discuss an ideal class period, an ideal week, and an ideal course
- Discuss the amount of technology that will be used and how that technology can be put to the best pedagogical use

How to compromise
- Prioritize topics and assignments most important to you
- Accept that not all assignments will be used and not all topics will be of equal interest to you and your colleague
- Remember to listen to your team teacher rather than just waiting for your next turn to talk: this is true in the classroom and in the planning process
- Read a book on teaching together and meet to discuss it

How to refine

- Set regular meetings, either immediately after class or at least once per week, to assess the success of the collaboration and to plan for the next class period/week
- Regularly ask students for feedback—either online or in class—after a few weeks, mid-semester, and at the end
- Start planning the next course while you are team teaching the current one and take good notes to help improve the next offering of the course

---

Adapted from the Magna 20-Minute Mentor program, *Is Team Teaching Right for Me?*

Class Participation Feedback Form

Maryellen Weimer, PhD

The following could be used on a form that provides feedback on participation as it is occurring in the classroom. Students could rate each item using a Likert-type scale, say five points with one being the low score and five the high score. The items ask for feedback on how participation is occurring in the class generally, not aspects of participation as it relates to them. However, the items could easily be worded to solicit feedback about individual perceptions.

- the amount of time devoted to participation in this class
- the extent to which student volunteer comments and are not called upon to participate
- the relevance and usefulness of the questions asked by students in this class
- the relevance and usefulness of comments contributed by students in this class
- the level of attention students are paying when another student is speaking
- the level of attention paid by the teacher to the student who is speaking
- the feedback provided students who participate by other students
- the feedback provided students who participate by the teacher
- the teacher's response to wrong or not very good answers
- the teacher's response to right and excellent answers
- the effectiveness of participation in this class at holding students' interest
- the effectiveness of participation in this class at clarifying confusing content
- the effectiveness of participation at introducing students to a variety of different viewpoints
- the level of comfort students feel when participating in this class

Adapted from the Magna 20-Minute Mentor program, *How Do I Get More Students to Participate in Class?*

About the Contributors

Kenneth L. Alford, PhD is a professor of church history and doctrine at Brigham Young University. After serving almost 30 years on active duty in the U.S. Army, he retired as a Colonel in 2008. Alford served in numerous assignments while on active military duty, including the Pentagon, eight years teaching computer science at the United States Military Academy at West Point, and four years as department chair and professor teaching strategic leadership at the National Defense University. He has published and presented on a wide variety of topics during his career.

Elizabeth Barkley, PhD is a professor of music history at Foothill College and holds a BA and MA from the University of California, Riverside, and a PhD from the University of California, Berkeley.

Kevin Brown, PhD is a professor at Lee University. He has published three books of poetry: *Liturgical Calendar: Poems* (Wipf and Stock); *A Lexicon of Lost Words* (winner of the Violet Reed Haas Prize for Poetry, Snake Nation Press); and *Exit Lines* (Plain View Press). He also has a memoir, *Another Way: Finding Faith, Then Finding It Again*, and a book of scholarship, *They Love to Tell the Stories: Five Contemporary Novelists Take on the Gospels*.

David Burrows, PhD is presently a provost and dean of the faculty at Lawrence University. He will be returning to teaching in June 2017 as a professor of psychology at Lawrence.

Rob Dornsife, PhD is a professor of English at Creighton University. He received Creighton University's highest student-selected teaching honor, the Robert F. Kennedy Student Award for Excellence in Teaching, presented at the Creighton University Spring

Commencement ceremony. Creighton's campus newspaper, *The Creightonian*, cited Dornsife (in a tie) as "Favorite Professor" in its "Best of CU" supplement.

Bonnie S. Farley-Lucas, PhD is a professor of communication at Southern Connecticut State University, and has nearly 30 years of experience as an organizational development consultant and trainer. She has presented more than 60 papers and workshops at regional, national, and international conferences. She earned a BA in communication from SCSU Honors College, an MS in organizational behavior from the University of Hartford, and a PhD from Ohio University.

Sydney Fulbright, PhD, MSN, RN, CNOR, is an associate professor in the College of Health Sciences at the University of Arkansas–Fort Smith.

Amy Getty, PhD is a professor of English at Grandview University.

Barbara Jacoby, PhD is faculty associate for leadership and community service-learning at the Adele H. Stamp Student Union–Center for Campus Life at the University of Maryland, College Park. In this role, she facilitates initiatives involving academic partnerships, service-learning, and civic engagement.

Rob Kelly is the former editor of *Academic Leader* and *Online Classroom* newsletters.

Marissa King is a professor of education. Currently she is a Yale National Fellow and wants every student to know the power of writing. She's grateful for collaborative Hesston College colleagues who reach across disciplines to make a difference for students.

Sarah M. Leupen, PhD is a senior lecturer at University of Maryland Baltimore County.

Karen Sheriff LeVan, PhD teaches in the English department at Hesston College in central Kansas. With zeal for writing identity across the lifespan, she currently researches and writes about the struggle for words in the 5th grade classroom, college writing culture, and older adult creative writing groups.

Claire Howell Major, PhD is a professor of higher education and chair of the department of educational leadership, technology, and policy at The University of Alabama in Tuscaloosa, Alabama. She teaches courses on college teaching, technology in higher education, reading research in the field of higher education, and qualitative research methods.

Nicki Monahan, MEd, is a faculty advisor in staff and organizational development at George Brown College, Toronto, Canada. She works directly with faculty, providing training, support, and consultation to help advance the college's strategic goal of "excellence in teaching and learning."

Alicja Rieger, PhD is an associate professor at Valdosta State University.

Patricia Stan, PhD is an associate professor of chemistry at Taylor University. She is an inorganic chemist with a specialty in organometallic synthesis. Teaching experience includes an inorganic class for chemistry majors, a team taught forensics class for non-majors and a large general chemistry class for non-majors called Chemistry for Living. Helping students see the connection between chemistry and other interests in their lives is one of the joys of teaching.

Suzanne M. Swiderski, PhD is an assistant professor at the University of Wisconsin, Parkside.

Roben Torosyan, PhD is director of teaching and learning (teaching philosophy; education) at Bridgewater State University (MA). He has facilitated 46 invited presentations at conferences and institutions including Harvard, Yale, Columbia and Brown. Specialties include critical and creative thinking, conflict, feedback, groups, time management.

Scott Warnock, PhD is an associate professor of English and director of the Writing Center and Writing Across the Curriculum at Drexel University.

Maryellen Weimer, PhD has edited *The Teaching Professor* newsletter since 1987 and writes the Teaching Professor blog each week on *Faculty Focus*. She is a professor emerita of teaching and learning at Penn State Berks and won Penn State's Milton S. Eisenhower award for distinguished teaching in 2005. She has published several books, including *Inspired College Teaching: A Career-Long Resource for Professional Growth* (Jossey-Bass, 2010), *Enhancing Scholarly Work on Teaching and Learning: Professional Literature that Makes a Difference* (Jossey-Bass, 2006), and *Learner-Centered Teaching: Five Key Changes to Practice* (Jossey-Bass, 2002).

Matthew P. Winslow, PhD is a professor of psychology at Eastern Kentucky University. Winslow is also the teaching enhancement coordinator for the department of psychology, and the coordinator of EKU's Faculty Innovator Program.

Additional Resources
from Magna Publications

BULK PURCHASES

To purchase multiple print copies of this book, please visit:
www.MagnaGroupBooks.com

MEMBERSHIPS/SUBSCRIPTIONS

Faculty Focus
www.facultyfocus.com
A free e-newsletter on effective teaching strategies for the college classroom.

The Teaching Professor Membership
www.TeachingProfessor.com
The Teaching Professor is an annual membership that reflects the changing needs of today's college faculty and the students they teach. This new fully online version of the newsletter that faculty have enjoyed for more than 30 years includes the best of the print version—great articles and practical, evidence-based insights—but also many new features including video, graphics, and links that make it an even more indispensable resource.

Academic Leader Membership
www.Academic-Leader.com
Academic Leader covers the trends, challenges, and best practices today's academic decision-makers. Members gain access to the latest thinking in academic leadership and learn how peers at other institutions are solving problems, managing change, and setting direction. New articles are published throughout the month.

CONFERENCES

The Teaching Professor Annual Conference
www.TeachingProfessorConference.com
This event provides an opportunity to learn effective pedagogical techniques, hear from leading teaching experts, and interact with colleagues committed to teaching and learning excellence. Join more than 1,000 educators from around the country.

Leadership in Higher Education Conference
www.AcademicLeadershipConference.com
The Leadership in Higher Education Conference provides higher-education leaders with an opportunity to expand leadership skills with proactive strategies, engaging networking, time-saving tips, and best practices. Attendees will hear from a roster of prestigious experts and nationally recognized thought leaders. A broad mix of plenary addresses, concurrent sessions, and timely roundtable discussions leave no topic untouched.

BOOKS

The Academic Leader's Handbook: A Resource Collection for College Administrators
https://www.amazon.com/dp/B0764KMC5Z
The Academic Leader's Handbook: A Resource Collection for College Administrators details an array of proven management strategies and will help further your achievements as a leader in higher education. Discover new leadership tools and insights at departmental, administrative, and executive levels.

The College Teacher's Handbook: A Resource Collection for New Faculty
https://www.amazon.com/dp/0912150688
The College Teacher's Handbook: A Resource Collection for New Faculty provides the essential tools and information that any new teacher in higher education needs to confidently lead a college classroom.

Essential Teaching Principles: A Resource Collection for Adjunct Faculty
https://www.amazon.com/dp/0912150246
This book provides a wealth of both research-driven and classroom-tested best practices to help adjuncts develop the knowledge and skills required to run a successful classroom. Compact and reader-friendly, this book is conveniently organized to serve as a ready reference whenever a new teaching challenge arises— whether it's refreshing older course design, overcoming a student's objection to a grade, or fine-tuning assessments.

Essential Teaching Principles: A Resource Collection for Teachers
https://www.amazon.com/dp/0912150580
This book serves as a quick and ready reference as you encounter the challenges of teaching college-level material in the high school classroom. For an AP or IB teacher, there's no better resource.

Faculty Development: A Resource Collection for Academic Leaders
https://www.amazon.com/dp/0912150661
Discover proven tips and insights, from top academic experts, that will help you enhance faculty development programming and training on your campus.

Flipping the College Classroom: Practical Advice from Faculty
https://www.amazon.com/dp/B01N2GZ61O
This collection is a comprehensive guide to flipping no matter how much—or how little—experience you have with it. If you are just getting started, you will learn where and how to begin. If you have been at it for a while, you will find new ideas to try and solutions to common challenges. Flipping the College Classroom: Practical Advice from Faculty is an invaluable resource that covers all the necessary territory.

Grading Strategies for the Online College Classroom: A Collection of Articles for Faculty
https://www.amazon.com/dp/0912150564
Do your grading practices accurately reflect your online students' performance? Do your assessment and feedback methods inspire learning? Are you managing the time you spend on these things—or is the workload overwhelming? *Grading Strategies for the Online College Classroom: A Collection of Articles for Faculty* can help you master the techniques of effective online grading—while avoiding some of the more costly pitfalls.

Helping Students Learn: Resources, Tools, and Activities for College Educators
https://www.amazon.com/dp/0912150602
This collection is packed with ideas, strategies, resources, activities, assignments, handouts, and more for teachers to use in the classroom to help their students become better at the very thing they are there to do: Learn.
Features of the book include: summaries of current research (with full citations); assignments or quizzes to use in the classroom; handouts to distribute to students; review and reflection worksheets at the end of every section; and thoughts and reflections from Maryellen Weimer.

Managing Adjunct Faculty: A Resource Collection for Administrators
https://www.amazon.com/dp/B01N2OVK5W
Chances are your adjunct population has been built on an ad hoc basis to fill instructional needs. As a result, your institution might not have a solid management framework to support them. That's a gap you can close with guidance from *Managing Adjunct Faculty: A Resource Collection for Administrators*. This invaluable guide offers an extensive review of best practices for managing an adjunct cohort and integrating them more fully into your campus community.

Teaching Strategies for the Online College Classroom: A Collection of Faculty Articles
https://www.amazon.com/dp/0912150483
Includes online teaching strategies ranging from building a successful start of the semester, fostering productive connections, managing challenging behavior in the online classroom, and enhancing student engagement.

Made in USA - Kendallville, IN
938486_9780912150611
02.12.2021 1813